THE THEOLOGY OF
MARTIN LUTHER

THE THEOLOGY OF MARTIN LUTHER

by

H. H. KRAMM, D.Phil. (Oxon)

*Minister of the German Lutheran Church
St. Mary - le - Savoy, London,
and of the Lutheran Congregation at Oxford*

WIPF & STOCK · Eugene, Oregon

Wipf and Stock Publishers
199 W 8th Ave, Suite 3
Eugene, OR 97401

The Theology of Martin Luther
By Kramm, H. H.
Copyright©1947 James Clarke & Co
ISBN 13: 978-1-60608-765-7
Publication date 6/1/2009
Previously published by James Clarke & Co, 1947

Copyright©James Clarke & Co1947
First English edition 1947 by James Clarke & Co
This edition published by arrangement with James Clarke & Co

CONTENTS

	PAGE
PREFACE	11
I. INTRODUCTION	13
1. Luther and Lutheranism	13
2. What was the central idea and main concern of Luther's reformation?	18
(a) The problem	18
(b) Misinterpretations	19
(c) Purely religious motive	21
3. Why did the Lutheran movement not remain a merely spiritual movement within the Church, but led to practical reforms, revolution of Church order and disruption of the organised Church?	25
4. Is Luther responsible for starting the "Reformation," or is it only the necessary outcome of a historic development?	29
5. Against whom did Luther fight?	31
6. Are Luther's theological views on the whole consistent during the time of his reformation activities?	31
II. THE DOCTRINE OF THE NATURE OF MAN	34
1. Human sin	34
2. The origin of the soul	38
3. Free will	39
4. The devil	41
5. Predestination	42
6. Ordinances of creation	42
III. THE DOCTRINE OF SALVATION	44
1. Person of Christ	44
2. Work of Christ	46
3. Justification	47
4. Faith	49
5. Historic faith (belief)	49
6. Saving faith	51

7. *Finitum capax infiniti*	52
8. Sacraments	55
9. Baptism	56
10. Absolution	57
11. The Lord's Supper	58
12. Law and Gospel	59
13. The letter and the spirit	62
14. Distinction between Law and Gospel	66

IV. THE CHURCH AS THE BODY OF CHRIST—THE MINISTRY — 68

1. What is the Church?	68
2. Visible and invisible Church	68
3. True Apostolic succession	70
4. Church divisions and Church unity	72
5. Valid ministries and broken "Apostolic Succession"	74
6. What is the ministry?	77
7. Ordination	81
8. Validity of lay celebrations	84
9. No degrees of the ministry—*iure divino*	85
10. An episcopacy—*iure humano*	87
11. Church constitutions, ceremonies and the Word of God	91
12. Luther as a liturgical reformer	96
13. *In statu confessionis nihil est adiaphoron*	99

V. ESCHATOLOGY — 102

VI. LUTHER AND THE BIBLE — 105

1. The principle of Re-formation	105
2. *Sola Scriptura*	107
3. The canon of the Bible	111
4. The Bible as "the Word of God"	116
5. Luther's interpretation of the Bible	120

VII. CHURCH AND STATE — 126

1. Introduction	126
2. By what power should the Church be governed?	128
3. Christ's One Body	132
4. Congregationalism?	134

5. *Ecclesiola in ecclesia* — 134
6. "State Church"? — 135
7. Emergency bishops — 138
8. The "Christian member" — 139
9. Is the term "State Church" defensible? — 140
10. Religious unity within a territory? — 141
11. *Cuius regio, eius religio* — 141
12. Religion and Politics — 142
13. Anti-Semitism? — 147
14. Conclusion — 149

To
Principal NATHANIEL MICKLEM, D.D.
and his colleagues of Mansfield College, Oxford,
in gratitude

(in the year of the fourth centenary of Luther's
death, 1946)

ABBREVIATIONS

Bekenntnisschriften = *Die Bekenntnisschriften der evangelisch-lutherischen Kirche, herausgegeben vom Deutschen Evangelischen Kirchenausschuss*, Berlin-Charlottenburg, 1930.
W.A. = *Weimarer Ausgabe:* Weimar edition of Luther's writings. *Dr. Martin Luther's Werke. Kritische Gesamtausgabe*, Vols. I–LIV, Weimar, 1883–1928.
Tischr. = *Tischreden*, contained in the *Weimarer Ausgabe*, Weimar, 1912–21 (6 vols.).
Briefw. = *Briefwechsel*, contained in the *Weimarer Ausgabe*, Weimar, 1930–8 (8 vols.), containing Luther's letters up to 1539; for the rest of the letters I used
de Wette = Luther's letters, ed. by de Wette.
Luther's prefaces to the various books of the Bible (*Vorreden*) are contained in *Die Deutsche Bibel*, at present available at Oxford, Vol. I–VII, Vol. IX, first Part (Weimar, 1906–39). For the benefit of the reader, I used a short edition which is more easily available, exact title given on p. 106.
Dtsch. Ev. Gesangbuch = *Deutsches Evangelisches Gesangbuch (Auslandsgesangbuch*, first published 1915, E. S. Mittler & Son, Berlin).

LITERATURE FREQUENTLY QUOTED

ELERT, WERNER, *Morphologie des Luthertums*, München, 1931.
HOLL, KARL, *Gesammelte Aufsätze zur Kirchengeschichte*, I., Luther (4th and 5th ed.), Tübingen, 1927.
KÖSTLIN, JULIUS, *Luther's Theologie in ihrer geschichtlichen Entwicklung und ihrem inneren Zusammenhange*. Stuttgart, 1901.
MCKINNON, JAMES, *Luther and the Reformation*, London, New York, Toronto, I, 1925; II, 1928; III, 1929; IV, 1930.
Popular Symbolics, ed. by Th. Engelden, W. Arndt, Th. Graebner, F. E. Mayer, St. Louis, 1934.
SASSE, HERMANN, *Was heisst lutherisch?* München, 1934. Translation: *Here We Stand*, New York and London, 1938.

PREFACE

IT will be readily understood that the limited space of this book does not allow of an even approximately complete exposition of Luther's theology. I have therefore chosen for more comprehensive treatment only three aspects of this theology, of which I assume that they will be of particular interest to the English-speaking world, i.e. (*a*) Luther's teaching on the Church and the ministry, (*b*) his teaching on the Bible, and (*c*) his teaching on the relation of Church and State. The chapters dealing with these subjects are to a certain extent based on my own studies in Luther's writings and contain numerous references to his own works and to specialised literature, which may be a guide to anybody who wishes to study the above-named subjects more closely. The other chapters are in the main based on the works of other scholars, particularly Köstlin, Elert and Holl. Of course they are highly condensed, and I am aware of the fact that I am laying myself open to criticism for over-simplification. This, however, was inevitable, and, on the other hand, this simplification may serve to bring out the main ideas even more clearly. These chapters contain only a small number of quotations of particularly interesting passages from Luther's writings; for a more complete collection of quotations I would refer the reader to the works of the three above-named scholars and to other literature quoted, e.g. McKinnon, Sasse, Drews, Heim and the American book, *Popular Symbolics*.

Owing to the limited space at my disposal, I was compelled to omit entirely some aspects of Luther's theology which I consider of great importance—in particular, his attitude to suffering and to prayer and devotional life. The significance of the devotional side of Luther's theology for the life of faith and for the ecumenical movement has been recognised more and more during the last few decades, not only by Protestants, but also by some Roman Catholics. "The fighting Luther wounds, . . . the praying Luther heals, the fighting Luther separates, the praying Luther unites," said the Roman Catholic Anton Fischer.[1] This side of Luther's theology would be an interesting study in itself, but it was impossible to give it the full treatment it deserves within the framework of this book.

I have tried to throw into relief the difference between Luther's creed and that of other denominations, because I thought this was in keeping with the purpose of this study, which is not to attack

[1] Quoted from F. Heiler, *Im Ringen um die Kirche*, München, 1931, pp. 204f.

other Churches, but to give a scientific and objective picture of Luther's theology, regardless of whether this theology is palatable to modern Christian circles or not. It is my firm belief that I am serving the ecumenical movement best by not covering up differences between Luther and the Lutherans on the one hand and the other Churches on the other, for only a clear recognition of differences can be the basis for an honest attempt to overcome them, or, if that is not yet practicable, such clear recognition will make it possible for the denominations to co-operate in spheres in which they already agree, or where doctrinal differences are of minor importance.

For the benefit of readers who are not familiar with the German language of the sixteenth century, I have adopted modern spelling when quoting passages from Luther and his contemporaries in German.

I gratefully acknowledge my indebtedness to Dr. N. Micklem and Mansfield College, Oxford, who have enabled me to do research work on Luther as well as to lecture on that subject; further, to the Chaplain of Mansfield College, the Rev. W. A. Whitehouse, who was good enough to help me over linguistic difficulties; finally, to Miss M. Pickering-Clarke and Dr. Ursula Behr for their help in linguistic and technical matters.

I

INTRODUCTION

1. *Luther and Lutheranism*

THE influence of the theology of Martin Luther is not limited to Lutherans only. It cannot be doubted that practically all sixteenth-century reformers were directly or indirectly influenced by Luther's ideas. This applies not only to Zwingli and Calvin, but also to theologians like Cranmer and to Bucer whose influence upon this country's reformation was in no way negligible. It is commonly known that John Wesley's conversion was the result of listening to Luther's thoughts, and it would be easy to add many other names.

But it is obvious that all these reformers only adopted part of Luther's theological conceptions. Other opinions of his were transformed by them and a good deal was more or less strongly rejected. The Calvinistic or the Wesleyan Churches are certainly clearly distinguishable from Lutheran Churches, in spite of many things which they have in common. It is perhaps even possible to say that Luther's negative influence, i.e. the opposition provoked by some of his ideas, was and is almost as great as his positive influence. In this sense Luther's theology influenced the sixteenth-century Anabaptists and Enthusiasts by the opposition it encountered, while even the Roman Catholic Church, by her wish to oppose Luther, was forced to re-examine her doctrine at the Council of Trent and to offer authoritative definitions in matters touched by Luther's reformation. There is a school of thought representing the opinion that Luther's influence forced all sixteenth-century Churches, friend and foe alike, to bring about some form of reformation in order to cope with the new situation which had arisen as a consequence of Luther's theology.[1]

The most direct and most visible result of Luther's theology, however, was the formation of so-called Lutheran Churches. But, to be correct, we shall have to make a distinction between "Luther's ideas" and "Lutheran ideas," the first expression meaning the conceptions set forth by Martin Luther himself, the second expression covering views held by the Lutheran Churches.[2] Many will think that both these terms describe identical views,

[1] H. Sasse, *Was heisst lutherisch?*, München, 1934, pp. 52ff. Transl.: *Here We Stand*, New York and London, 1938, p. 54.
[2] *ibid.*, pp. 21ff., 67–70, 88ff. Transl., pp. 22ff., 67–70, 91f.

and this is right to a very large extent. Non-Lutherans like to point out that the authority as enjoyed by Luther among Lutherans by far exceeds the authority of other reformers in *their* Churches. Calvinists may sometimes ironically refer to the journeys of many Lutherans to Wittenberg and to interpret them as "pilgrimages" in order to visit the "Holy Tomb of Luther" while Calvin's tomb is no longer to be found. Some Roman Catholics like to say: in our Church all Popes together form one infallible authority while in the Lutheran Church Luther himself is alone infallible. It is certainly true that Luther's authority among Lutherans exceeds the authority of English Reformers among the Christians in England. The German schoolboy almost takes it for granted that a non-Roman Church is based on the authority of a reformer, and as a consequence of this idea many Germans quite seriously believe Henry VIII to be the Anglican Reformer.

While we have to admit the unique authority held by Luther in his Church, we must not forget the fact that by definition and law a "Lutheran" is not bound to share all views ever proclaimed by Luther. By definition and law a Lutheran is a Christian who accepts the Augsburg Confession, i.e. who believes this Confession to be the proper interpretation of Holy Scripture. In the Augsburg Diet in 1530 Emperor Charles V asked the followers of Luther for an official document—setting forth their views, their doctrine and grievances. They produced the Augsburg Confession (*Confessio Augustana*) written mainly by Luther's friend Melanchthon with the co-operation and advice of other theologians. Luther approved the Confession and found that it expressed his views correctly. He added that the tone of the Confession was more moderate than the style used by himself in his own writings. But I do not think that this remark represents a criticism of the substance of the Confession. Later on he treats the Augsburg Confession as an official document of the Church.[1]

Soon after that Augsburg Diet the official charters and documents referred to the Lutherans as "people related to the Augsburg Confession" (*Augsburger Confessions-Verwandte* and similar descriptions).[2]

---

[1] *Briefwechsel*, No. 1,568, May 15th, 1530; on the preparations for the Augsburg Confession, its authority and Luther's judgment, cf. J. T. Müller, *Die Symbolischen Bücher der evang.-luth. Kirche*, 10 ed. 1907. pp. livff., *Die Bekenntnissschriften der Evangelisch-Lutherischen Kirche, herausgegeben vom Deutschen Evangelischen Kirchenausschuss*, Berlin-Charlottenburg, 1930 (quoted throughout this book as *Bekenntnisschriften*), pp. xviff.; *Briefw.* Nos. 1,564, 1565, May 11th, 1530.

[2] About the terms *Adherents of the Augsburg Confession, Lutheran, Evangelical Reformed, Protestant*, etc., cf. H. Sasse, *Was heisst lutherisch?*, pp. 11ff., 23ff. Here *We Stand*, pp. 11ff., pp. 23ff.

Therefore it is fair to say that a Lutheran Church is a Church adopting the Augsburg Confession. This means at the same time accepting the Bible as the fundamental authority of faith, as *norma fidei*.

For the Bible is recognised by the Augsburg Confession as the fundamental authority, and the three early Church Creeds, the Apostolic, Nicene, and Athanasian Creeds, are by implication recognised as a correct interpretation of Holy Scripture.[1]

In 1555 religious peace in Germany was re-established by the so-called "Religious Peace of Augsburg" (*Augsburger Religionsfriede*) after the strifes of the Reformation. But this agreement did not bring about general religious freedom, but only a settlement according to which the different German territories were given the choice of either remaining in the Catholic Church under the Pope or of basing their religion on the Augsburg Confession. In many states deciding for the latter alternative, and (earlier or later) also in some non-German states all State officials were bound to "confess the pure Evangelical Doctrine as set forth in the Bible, the three Ecumenical Creeds of the early Church and the Augsburg Confession" (Sweden). Still to-day the Government Ministers in Sweden, half of the Norwegian Government and all Scandinavian kings are bound to accept the Augsburg Confession.[2] Through these and similar developments the Augsburg Confession became a part of German and Scandinavian State law. But the long official title of the Churches adhering to it as "relatives of the Augsburg Confession" was in popular use replaced by the word "Lutheran," and many of these Churches adopted this term in their official documents.

Later on the Augsburg Confession was explained by a number of additional Lutheran Confessions (*Bekenntnisschriften*). Emperor Charles V refused to recognise the Augsburg Confession when it was presented to him. He alleged that the party opposing the Confession was right. For this reason, an "Apologia" written by Melanchthon was added in order to explain and to defend the disputed opinions. A few years later the Lutherans were asked to plead their cause on a general Church Council. Preparing for this Council, Lutheran theologians—including Luther himself—met at Schmalkalden in 1537 and drew up a document stating and explaining the points which they intended to raise at the Council. The proposed Council did not materialise, but

---

[1] The Nicene Creed is expressly recognised, Augsburg Confession, Art I; about the recognition of the Early Church creeds in Lutheranism, cf. W. Elert, *Morphologie des Luthertums*, München, 1931, I, pp. 176ff.

[2] Norway: *Kongeriget Norges Grundlov* (Constitution), § 2, § 4. Sweden: *Kyrkolagen* (Church Law) of 1686, cpt. 1, § 1, § 2, Constitution of June 6th, 1809, § 2, § 4. Denmark: *Grundloven* (Constitution), § 3, § 5.

the so-called "Schmalkalden Articles" became in the course of time part of the official Lutheran Confessions. The same applies to Luther's "Long and Short Catechism." And about thirty years after Luther's death it was felt that certain contradictions and theological disputes among the Lutherans themselves and between Lutherans and Calvinists made it desirable to clarify the position and to decide these disputes in one more Confession. After complicated theological negotiations, a long book emerged, the so-called *Formula Concordiae* (Formula of Concord).

While all Lutheran Churches accepted the Augsburg Confession and Luther's Short Catechism, not all of them adopted all the additional Articles and Confessions.

It is obvious that in the course of history Lutheran ministers, while formally accepting these "Confessional" writings, did not always take them too seriously, and at some time and in some places the Church authorities made no real efforts to force the ministers to bring their doctrine and Church work into agreement with the Confessions. This happened especially during the time of enlightenment and rationalism. On the other hand, attempts were made from time to time, both by the Church governments and by ministers and laymen, to stress the importance of the Augsburg Confession and the other Confessions for the Church. It is probably safe to say that during the last decades the authority of the Confessions has been growing in German theology. The fourth centenary of the Augsburg Confession in 1930 was made the occasion for celebrations; a new edition of the Lutheran Confessions was made, and theologians and laymen studied the Augsburg Confession afresh. The recent German Church conflict after 1933 re-enforced the authority of the Confessions as documents of legal importance. When *Reichsbischof* Müller and other National-Socialist Church authorities introduced un-Christian principles into the Church (dictatorship, racial discrimination, abolition of Pauline doctrines, objection to the Old Testament) many ministers disobeyed, and, threatened with dismissal and loss of their salaries, they claimed before the courts that the Augsburg Confession and other Confessions forbade them to accept these principles. As the validity of these Confessions in the German Evangelical Churches was recognised by State law, many judges admitted that the opposing ministers were right in refusing obedience to these Nazi principles in the sphere of the Church.[1]

As we have seen previously, it is obvious that the general contents of the Lutheran Confessions and the main conceptions of

[1] Cf. A. S. Duncan-Jones (Dean of Chichester), *The Struggle for Religious Freedom in Germany*, London, 1938, pp. 105ff.

Martin Luther himself are identical. And yet—this was our starting point—Lutherans are not bound to share all views ever expressed by Luther. Many will believe that Luther's ideas are not always quite consistent and that some of his opinions seem to change in different periods of his life. The Confessions, accepted by representative Lutheran Church assemblies or theologians, represent a more balanced view, and many young Lutheran candidates for ordination will put their signature to the Augsburg Confession with a much easier heart than to the seventy or eighty big volumes of the Weimar Edition of Luther's writings. Others, however, claim, on the contrary, that the original depth and strength of Luther's theological thinking were lost through the simplification and moderation achieved by the Confessions,[1] and some regard with suspicion and criticism the influence of Melanchthon in the composition of some Confessions.

The term "Lutherans" was already used in Luther's lifetime. Luther objected to this term, certainly not as a result of any special modesty, which he did not possess if his doctrine was at stake, but just because he thought that his theology contained the only right and true Christian doctrine and that there was no way of being a real Christian except by being a "Lutheran." He did not desire that the true Church should be called by a name which sounded like a sectarian label.[2] If he needed a term for describing his followers as distinct from "Popish people" (*Papişten*) he preferred the word "Evangelicals," followers of the Gospel. Later, however, he acquiesced in the use of his name, and he himself says: "We so-called Lutherans."[3] In addition, the term "Protestants" was used for the Lutherans, and it is believed that this term first was derived from the Lutheran minority at the Speyer Reichstag in 1529 which "protested" against the resolutions of the Popish majority. For some time the expressions "Evangelical," "Protestant," and "Lutheran" were used side by side. Later, however, the "Calvinists," officially called "the Church Reformed according to the Word of God" (shortened to: "Reformed Church"), adopted the names "Evangelical" and "Protestant" as well, and to-day there is a general confusion of terms on the Continent, further increased by the fact that in Old Prussia and elsewhere Lutherans and Calvinists concluded a union. When asking for the denomination of a particular church in Germany you will probably receive the answer: "This church is Evangelical"

[1] "*der entschiedene Schritt über das Luthertum der Augustana hinaus*," Karl Barth, *Das Wort Gottes und die Theologie*, München, 1924, p. 211; F. Hildebrandt, *Est, Das Lutherische Prinzip*, Göttingen, 1931, p. 3.
[2] *W.A.*, 8, 685, 4.
[3] *W.A.*, 31, I, 209, 16; cf. *W.A.*, 30, II, 541, 5; 30, III, 446ff.

B

(*evangelisch*) or "Protestant." You will probably need further enquiries to find out whether the church is Lutheran or vinist, and frequently you will find that the Church is a promise between both.

It is important to note that the English terms "Evangelical" and "Protestant" do not quite correspond to the German meaning of these terms.

2. *What was the central idea and main concern of Luther's reformation?*

(a) *The Problem*

Luther's reformation has—at least in Germany and Scandinavia—affected and changed all spheres of life. It affected doctrine, religious life, preaching, liturgy, music and art; it affected Church order, constitution and finance; it affected the political sphere, especially the relation between Church and State, but also between territorial princes and the German Emperor; it affected schools and universities, training and moral life of ministers and laymen; and it affected many other spheres, including the creation of a commonly used "high German" language.

It is obvious that many of these changes were only the accidental consequences of Luther's reformation, not its main concern. The creation of a high German language was a more or less necessary consequence of Luther's activities as a religious reformer. His reformation being mainly based on Scriptures, he wanted all people to be able to read the Bible. Therefore the Bible had to be edited in a popular German edition. But there was no common German language. When Luther wanted to write a letter to the Mayor and City Council of Lubeck or Brunswick he had to ask his friend Bugenhagen to translate his letter from Saxonian into Low German, unless he preferred to write in Latin. Numerous misunderstandings happened in theological discussions, e.g. some theologians understood the word *Jungfrau* as meaning a virgin, and the word *Magd* as describing a girl in domestic service, while other theologians understood the same words just the other way round, because they were used in a different sense in different parts of Germany.[1]

Luther, when translating the Bible, simply took that German dialect which seemed to him most suitable, and somewhere in the middle between Northern and Southern German language (the language of the Saxonian chancellery at Meissen). As everybody was going to read the Bible in Luther's translation and as this

[1] K. Aner, *Kirchengeschichte III* (Göschenband, 987), Berlin and Leipzig, 1929, p. 95, note 2. On Reformation and Culture, *ibid.*, pp. 94-103, and K. Holl, *Gesammelte Aufsätze zur Kirchengeschichte I, Luther*, Tübingen, 1927⁵, pp. 8-543.

Bible language became the official Church and school language, in a very short time all Germans learned this High German language of Luther's Bible side by side with their own dialect. It can, however, not be denied that the creation of this language was but a consequence of Luther's work, not his main concern.

(b) *Misinterpretations*

But what *was* his main concern, his chief motive? The most varying answers can be heard. There are quite superficial interpretations of Luther's work. Some people think that Luther's main aim was the abolition of Papacy and episcopal Church constitution, or that his motive was a Puritan anti-ceremonial spirit. Others think that he tried to make Christianity more worldly and therefore fought ascetic and monastic tendencies. Others tried to interpret Luther's main concern as an attempt to establish Erastianism and to make the Churches blindly obedient slaves of the State. Two interpretations have been very popular during our time. One is the attempt to explain Luther's work as "Germanization of Christianity," i.e. its adaptation to the mystic Germanic national soul with all its well-known qualities. Many people who abhor German mentality and Lutheranism alike agree in this interpretation with the Nazi Christians who have accepted it generally. The other modern attempt of interpretation is to understand Luther from psychological motives only.[1] But even if Luther's action could be explained as a result of a rather abnormal psychology, this would not explain his importance for millions of Christians in many countries during four centuries.

All these quoted interpretations more or less miss the point and can only be maintained by persons with a great amount of ignorance about the history of the Reformation. The reader will find the details for this judgment in the later passages of this book.

Finally, there only remain two serious alternatives:

(i) Was Luther's main motive the attempt to introduce sound learning, reasonable thinking and honest scholarship into the Church, i.e. was he primarily a son of Renaissance and Humanism?

(ii) Or was his main motive purely religious, a Biblical reformation and revival of the Church?

It is obvious that Luther strongly emphasised the necessity for learning.[2] He was a university professor and proud of being a

[1] P. Reiter, *Martin Luthers Umwelt, Charakter und Psychose*, Bd. I, Kopenhagen, 1937 (quoted in *Junge Kirche*, 1938, Heft 19, pp. 828f.).

[2] See below, p. 144, note 3.

Doctor of Holy Scriptures. The Lutherans very early introduced difficult examinations as a condition for ordination;[1] they stressed the importance of the divinity degrees for the Church and revived them at Wittenberg where these degrees had been neglected;[2] they demanded instruction and knowledge as a necessary condition before admitting a layman to the Lord's Table.[3] In many writings Luther emphasised the need for establishing schools for all Christian youths.[4] The old languages were for him the "sheath containing the sword of the spirit."[5] A knowledge of Greek and Hebrew in addition to Latin was (and on the whole still is) demanded for the most humble Lutheran village curate. Therefore it was most easy for superficial observers to imagine that this line was Luther's main concern, that he primarily was a son of the Renaissance and of Humanism, a disciple of Erasmus of Rotterdam, and that his religious views and doctrines are only the result of applying reason and the scholarship available in *his* days to the Church of *his* days.

If this interpretation of Luther's reformation were true we should go on to say that the reason and scholarship of *his* time was not yet as far advanced as that of *our* time. The real Lutheran therefore is the man who constantly introduces reason and scholarship of the most modern type into the Church. We have to continue and perhaps to finish the work which was only begun by Luther. And if all doctrines that Luther held should prove indefensible before the scholarship of our days, if Luther's interpretation of the Bible should now prove quite obsolete, we should fulfil Luther's own desire by accepting the consequences and by abolishing all these unreasonable things, even if Luther himself had believed in them. Catholics who criticise this attitude and Protestant modernists who would approve of it often are united in summing up: Luther was the first modernist, Lutherism does not know any dogmatic and unchangeable doctrines. The principle of "re-formation" generally and of Lutherism in particular would then mean: The Church has to be remodelled from decade to decade, according to the spirit and reason of the time. This demand has frequently been heard in Lutheran Churches since the time of enlightenment and rationalism, it was reinforced by "higher criticism" and by forces which demanded "progressive changes" in the Church of modern times. And, last but not least, it was violently repeated by the Nazis.

One could make out quite a strong case for this interpretation

---

[1] P. Drews, *Die Ordination, Prüfung und Lehrverpflichtung der Ordinanden Wittenberg 1535* (Programm der Universität Giessen), Giessen, 1905.
[2] *W.A.*, 39, I, 40ff.; 39, II, 176. [3] See below, p. 50f.
[4] e.g. *W.A.*, 15, 15ff. [5] *W.A.*, 15, 38.

but for Luther's conflict with Erasmus and the Humanists. History has made it easier for us to decide this question. Luther's complete break with Erasmus quite definitely indicates that the above summarised line of thought is not Luther's line at all. And Erasmus' judgment, *"Ubicumque regnat Lutheranismus, ibi literarum est interitus,"* was not quite just but showed that the "King of the Humanists" was quite aware of the fact that the spirit of Luther's reformation was totally alien to himself.[1] Luther is primarily a religious reformer based on the Bible. Not reason but the Bible is his starting point. His attitude to reason is ambiguous. There are three things which Luther praises and insults alternatively: the lawyers,[2] the princes[3] and reason.[4] He is prepared to accept help from lawyers, princes and reason if they promote what he thinks to be the pure interpretation of the Bible. In his defence before the Diet at Worms in 1521 he appeals to *ratio evidens* in addition to the authority of Scriptures. He is also prepared to leave to the lawyers, princes and reason all those neutral spheres of life which, as he thinks, are irrelevant for religion.[5] But he strongly opposes all three of them, if they in any way try to interfere with the demands and doctrines of the Bible as he interprets them. Then he bitterly complains about the lawyers who spoil everything, he uses words against the princes which no university professor who wanted to stay in office could safely use in our days, and he fights against the "great whore," reason.

(c) Purely Religious Motive

The only starting point for Luther of those activities which resulted in his Reformation was his personal religious experience, his discovery of what is called "justification by faith alone" or "by grace alone." What this meant to him can only be understood by us if we try to grasp the meaning of the terrible conflict in Luther's mind before the discovery of this religious principle.[6] He was longing for the peace of his soul. We cannot make out definitely what forces were active to drive the young promising Master of Arts in Erfurt University, who was just preparing himself to read for the degree of a Doctor of Law, to abandon all his plans and—in spite of the strong disapproval of his father[7]—to

---

[1] O. Flake, *Ulrich von Hutten*, Berlin, 1929, pp. 126ff., 337–54. *Tischr.* 37, 173, 352, 432, 452, 463, 466, 468, 494, 3,795, 3,963, 4,028. Cf. McKinnon, *Luther and the Reformation*, III, 211–73.
[2] *Tischr.*, 109, 149, 3,496, 3,690, 3,793, 4,135
[3] See below, p. 133.   [4] See below, p. 109f.   [5] See below, pp. 145ff.
[6] For the following pages, cf. Holl, *op. cit.*, pp. 15–35; Aner, *op. cit.*, pp. 12–22.
[7] *Tischr.*, 623, 3,556A.

enter the monastery of the Augustinian Hermits in Erfurt, known for its most severe discipline and the rigid enforcement of its rules. He observed his hard duties scrupulously. It has been said that the young Master of Arts was given specially hard tasks in the monastery so as to humiliate him. This is probably legendary, but the ordinary rules of the monastery were extremely hard. Fasts, cold, and night-watches undermined his health and created psychological depressions. But his deepest afflictions cannot be explained as having had purely physical causes. He was pursued by the fear of God the Judge. He was not satisfied with himself and his good works, and he was terrified by his never-ceasing afflictions. It is wrong to interpret these afflictions as carnal temptations only. He himself said in later years: "In the monastery I never cared for material possessions or women, but my heart trembled and fluttered for God's grace. For I had strayed from faith and could not help thinking that I had provoked God's wrath and had to propitiate Him by good works."[1]

He found no consolation in the daily confession of his sins and in receiving sacramental absolution. It may be difficult for people of our day to imagine the violent force of such conflicts. He describes them a few years later in this way:

"I knew a man [meaning himself] who had to suffer these ordeals frequently, even though only for a few moments, but such tremendous and infernal ordeals that no tongue could speak them, no pen could write them and no one could believe them who had not experienced them. If they had lasted, or lasted for half an hour only, nay even for the tenth part of an hour, this man would have utterly perished and all his bones would have been burnt to cinders. In these moments God seems to be terrible in His wrath and with Him the whole creation. There is no way out, no consolation neither within (this man's soul) nor without, but all things accuse.

. . . . .

"And he does not even dare to say: O Lord, rebuke me not in thine anger. In such moments the soul, astonishingly, cannot believe that it is possible ever to be saved. . . ."[2]

The first man to help and to console him was his superior, Johan von Staupitz,[3] who taught him that the proper starting

---

[1] Sermon held December 7th, 1539, on Matt. xxiv.; *Tischr.*, 121.

[2] *W.A.*, 1, 557f. About "Luther's spiritual conflict," see McKinnon, *op. cit.*, I, 90–130.

[3] *Tischr.*, 94, 173, 526.

point for penitence was not torturing one's own body and soul but loving God.

"This word, Luther said, stuck within me like the pointed arrow of a strong man, and at once I started comparing it with those scriptural passages that treat the question of penitence. And behold, what a joyous game! From all sides the passages came to my assistance, smiled upon this interpretation and took its part. Thus it happened that the word penitence, which I had considered the bitterest word in the Scriptures, now became the sweetest and dearest word to me."[1]

The decisive experience, however, was what is known as his *Turmstubenerlebnis*, i.e. his experience in his room in the tower of Wittenberg Monastery.[2] He had taken up residence in this monastery at his superior's command in order to lecture at Wittenberg University. This *Turmstubenerlebnis* probably took place sometime in 1512 or 1513. The exact date is unknown.[3] What is known is the fact that Luther, preparing his lectures on the Psalms which were due to start in August, 1513, was struck by Ps. xxxi. 2, "Deliver me in *thy* righteousness." Up to then he had thought that God's righteousness was that of a judge who, by His righteousness, was forced to punish evil, and Luther had been depressed because he felt that his good works were in no way sufficient to reconcile God. The fact that the psalm quoted God's righteousness as something delivering and helping us rather than terrifying us made him read St. Paul's letter to the Romans, where he learned that God's righteousness was a gift to us, not a merciless claim against us. Rom. i. 16f. became the key to his new understanding of the Bible:

"For I am not ashamed of the Gospel of Christ: For it is the power of God unto salvation to everyone that believeth; to the Jew first, and also to the Greek. For therein is the righteousness of God revealed from faith to faith as it is written: The just shall live by faith." This passage made Luther say: "Here I felt myself to be born again and to enter Paradise itself through its open gates. There the whole face of Holy Scripture appeared to me different."[4]

[1] Letter to Staupitz, May 30th, 1518.
[2] "*Das Urerlebnis*" in Elert, *op. cit.*, I, 15–25; *Tischr.*, 4,007, 5,247, 5,518, 5,553.
[3] H. G. Voigt, "*Die entscheidendste Stunde in Luthers religiöser Entwicklung, ihre Oertlichkeit, Zeit und Bedeutung*" (*Zeitschrift für Kirchengeschichte der Provinz Sachsen*, XXIV), 1928; for details of literature see Elert, *op. cit.*, I, 15, note I; cf. McKinnon, *op. cit.*, I, 131–56.
[4] Latin Preface to the Complete Edition of Luther's *Works*, 1545.

This belief—generally known as the "justification by grace alone"—is certainly Luther's main concern. Everybody who realises the depth of his previous conflicts will understand that the detection of the "justification by grace" meant to him the gate of Paradise, was the decisive event of his life and the starting point of all his thinking, feeling and praying, and especially of all his interpretation of the Bible. It is obvious that St. Paul's Letter to the Romans had influenced him particularly strongly—for instance, passages like Rom. iii. 23:

"For all have sinned and come short of the glory of God, being justified freely by his grace through the redemption that is in Jesus Christ";

but one has to bear in mind that he interprets the *entire* Bible in the sense of his justification by grace, without regard to the issue raised by modern attempts to distinguish between the theology of the Synoptics and that of St. Paul. For him, the Psalms, Prophets and many Old Testament passages, all share the same opinion of justification by grace with the Synoptics, St. Paul, St. John and St. Peter.

This approach to Scripture illustrates to us the main feature of Luther's thinking. As his great Scripture discovery of the justification by grace alone had saved him from depression and despair and made him a happy man, this experience was the unalterable and indisputable starting point for him. All other authorities in the Church were judged by one measure only: what is their attitude to justification by grace—or, as Luther prefers to put it, "the Gospel"? Justification by grace and the Gospel were to him one and the same thing. If a book of the Bible supported his doctrine of justification by grace especially strongly, as, for instance, St. Paul's Letter to the Galatians, Luther praises the book above all. He says: "This Letter is my favourite Epistle to whom I am married, it is my Kate von Bora [the name of his wife]."[1] If Luther finds books in the Bible which appear not to lay special stress on this doctrine, he either treats these books as writings of less central importance or tries to interpret them according to his doctrine of justification (see below).

If we want to understand Luther's activities as a reformer, we have to note these two principles:

(1) The experience that man is saved by grace alone or by faith alone, is Luther's fundamental experience, the unalterable starting point of all his thinking and teaching.

[1] *Tischr.*, 146.

(2) If this doctrine is contradicted by any other authority, Luther is quite definitely convinced that not he but this authority is wrong. Not for a single moment does he doubt the infallible truth of his doctrine and experience on justification.

As it happened, several authorities contradicted *his* doctrine of justification. In the course of the years it became increasingly clear that the Pope, the monks, the liturgy of the Mass, the bishops and canon law, and finally the Emperor and the authority of the Reich would oppose and fight Luther's doctrine.

As he did not doubt for a moment the infallible truth of this doctrine, he was bound to draw the only alternative conclusion: the Pope and the monks, the liturgy of the Mass, the bishops and canon law, the Emperor and the Reich were wrong—and he, Luther himself, and his doctrine were right, even *if the whole world* were on the side of the Pope's bull against Luther, for this bull condemns the Gospel.[1] So Luther became a reformer.

3. *Why did the Lutheran movement not remain a merely spiritual movement within the Church, but led to practical reforms, revolution of Church order and disruption of the organised Church?*

There exists in some circles a rather naïve idea about Luther's reforming activities. This idea suggests that Luther started by objecting to certain parts of the Church constitution, did not like Pope, incense, monks and the celibacy of the clergy, and therefore thought of ways to abolish them. But primarily he was not a reformer of constitutions, rituals and organisations. Primarily he was a man preaching the main religious experience of his life: man is saved, is justified in the eyes of God by grace alone through faith. Only little by little he becomes aware of the practical consequences of his doctrine.

The first conflict arose with the Dominican monks, especially with Tetzel, in connection with the question of indulgences. Some of the parishioners of Wittenberg availed themselves of the possibility of acquiring indulgences, for payment, from Tetzel, who in 1517 was active in the vicinity of Wittenberg. Luther realised that this practice of selling indulgences constituted a denial of his doctrine on justification. The idea held by many people at that time and reflected in Luther's famous 95 Sentences (*Thesen*)— namely, the idea that the forgiveness of sins and salvation could be purchased for cash is certainly an unfair interpretation of the Catholic doctrine as to indulgences.

[1] *W.A.*, 7, 294; cf. McKinnon, *op. cit.*, II, 182–221.

Luther was not ignorant about the official Church doctrine on indulgences and even in many of his later writings (especially in 1520) he showed he knew how to distinguish between official Church doctrine and popular misuse.[1] Fairminded Catholic scholars would admit, however, that the practice and behaviour of some monks charged with the selling of indulgences was bound to lead to misunderstanding in the popular mind. The behaviour of Tetzel seems to have been specially shameful, as part of the money collected by him was used to repay the debts of an archbishop to Fugger Bankers in Augsburg. Officials of this bank, therefore, controlled Tetzel's activities. It is difficult to prove that the slogan quoted in Luther's 95 Sentences was *not* used by Tetzel: "As soon as the money is heard to drop into the box the soul [of the dead person for whom the money is given] will jump out of purgatory into heaven." At any rate, Tetzel's preaching was quite on these lines.

When Luther attacked the practice of indulgences by nailing his famous 95 Sentences on the door of Wittenberg Castle Church,[2] basing his attack on his views concerning justification, he in no way felt guilty of attacking the Catholic Church or the Pope. The door of that Church was the official notice board of the University and Luther hoped that his 95 Sentences would start an academic discussion on indulgences. When, however, this act and other activities of Luther led to a major Church conflict, Luther recognised that his views on justification were bound, not only to condemn Tetzel's misuse, but sooner or later to question the whole institution of indulgences.[3] And when it became obvious that Pope Leo X did not support Luther, but denied his theory of justification, then, as a matter of course, Luther drew the conclusion: My doctrine and the Pope's doctrine contradict each other. My doctrine is right—there is no doubt whatever. Conclusion: the Pope is wrong. And the fact that Pope Leo X was obviously wrong caused him to question the whole institution of the Papacy. But his main concern remained the doctrine of justification; the question of the Papacy was but one consequence— even if a most important one—arising from the proclamation of his doctrine. The Papacy stood in the way of "the Gospel"—as he put it—and this fact he had to face. Therefore for him the Pope became the Anti-Christ.

All his practical reforms were but the consequence of his religious concern to proclaim justification by grace in word and

---

[1] *W.A.*, 6, 548f.; cf. McKinnon, *op. cit.*, I, 281–305.
[2] *W.A.*, 1, 233ff.
[3] cf. Luther's writings on indulgences in 1517 (*W.A.*, 1, 233ff.) and 1518 (*W.A.*, 1, 243ff.); cf. McKinnon, *op. cit.*, II, 1–36.

action. On questions of Church order and ceremony, Luther was prepared to make very far-reaching concessions to the practice of his time. Friend and foe agree that he had a conservative tendency. But a very important development emerged: the purely religious concern, the preaching and teaching of a particular religious doctrine, was bound to lead to an enormous revolution inside the visible church organisation, a development of which Luther and his friends only became conscious in course of time.

Luther's conception of justification by grace was bound to raise the whole issue of eucharistic sacrifice, of masses for the dead, or for special guilds and corporations, and of the position of the priest as a mediator offering sacrifices to God. In this way the main foundations of the ecclesiastical practice of his day became subject to criticism, not forgetting the issue concerning indulgences which had provoked the conflict. Luther's teaching and the Church order which was inconsistent with it could not exist peacefully side by side. The day was bound to come when one fell victim to the other.

It is typical of Luther's conservative attitude that at first he himself did not commence practical reforms. He was primarily the preacher and teacher. But when the excommunicated and outlawed Luther was in hiding in Wartburg Castle and in serious danger, 1521-2, others started to alter the ritual in Wittenberg. His disciples knew how to draw the inference of their master's teaching. The conservative Luther thought they went much too far; he condemned the violence of their actions and was disgusted with the riots and tumults accompanying them. But he could not ignore the obvious fact that his proclaiming justification by grace was bound to lead to practical alterations in the Church life of those days. While Luther tried to persuade his disciples to keep to the customary ceremonies as much as possible and use restraint, he had to admit that they were not unreasonable in omitting those prayers and ceremonies which to all appearances were inconsistent with the doctrine of justification by grace alone. This concerned, in the first place, all parts of the liturgy which hinted at the character of the Mass as earning for us a merit before God ("meritorious" character of the Mass) or at the Eucharistic sacrifice. As therefore in many places the old ceremonies could no longer be kept as they were, Luther and his friends were urged to make alternative liturgical proposals. Luther had to suggest outlines for new prayer books consistent with his doctrine, and he did so by publishing a draft of a Latin prayer book in 1523, and a German one in 1526. Thus began his interference in questions of Church order and with the liturgical legislation, and thus also his encroachments on the authority of the Bishops and even of the Pope.¹

This liturgical reform at once led to complete chaos and breakdown of the financial system of the Church. Most of the money constituting the income of the Church had been given either by private persons who wanted to secure Masses for their dead relatives or by guilds and corporations, e.g. the tailors', shoemakers', fishermen's, etc., who wanted a priest to say Mass every morning in favour of their guild or trade. In many German city churches there were twenty or more altars for these purposes, and many relics of such altars can still be seen to-day. Many priests—I think probably the majority—received their stipends under the obligation to say Mass for these various purposes. Therefore, at the same moment in which this practice of the Mass was abolished, there collapsed also the main source of the income of the Church. Under the influence of Luther's doctrine, this happened in the greater part of Germany. Thousands of priests and canons had to give up saying Mass, which, till then, had brought them their means of living. Charitable institutions became superfluous and places of pilgrimage lost their importance. Monasteries and convents died out more or less quickly, as monastic life was rightly or wrongly interpreted as a way of winning salvation by human effort, by ascetic life and good works, challenging the doctrine of justification by grace. All this was bound to have tremendous financial consequences. Those who had given money for the maintenance of Masses wanted it back, while the greed of certain noblemen and secular authorities also claimed the Church money. Something had to be done at once and Luther had to make proposals as to how this property could best be used for religious and charitable purposes, how it could be prevented from being wasted or stolen.² Thus again he could not help interfering in questions of ecclesiastical administration. The abolition of celibacy was but an obvious consequence of his ideas.³ Here, too, others took the first practical steps. Luther himself married only in 1525. The support of married ministers with their families raised new financial problems.

¹ On the whole subject, cf. *W.A.*, 12, 35ff., 205ff., 19, 72ff.; L. Fendt, *Der Lutherische Gottesdienst des sechzehnten Jahrhunderts*, München, 1923, esp. pp. 85ff., 101ff.; cf. McKinnon, *op. cit.*, III, 34–46; 68–79; 102–17.
² e.g. *W.A.*, 12, 11ff.; *Briefw.*, Nos. 950, 1,766, 3,312, App. to No. 1,420. Those priests who lost their income through the Reformation ought to be treated kindly and receive a stipend from these funds. Luther does not want them to suffer hunger, *W.A.*, 18, 535, and many letters, e.g. *Briefw.*, Nos. 866, 983. They should not be "converted" to Lutheranism by external pressure; they ought to have time to make up their mind and to be provided for in the meantime. *Briefw.*, No. 1,425.
³ See below, p. 54, note 1.

No wonder that those bishops who supported the Pope and the existing Church order considered Lutheranism to be a most dangerous heresy. The bishops thus refused ordination to Lutheran-minded candidates for the ministry[1] and some demanded the signing of a written obligation never to marry, nor to support Lutheran ideas.[2] As a consequence, the Lutherans were forced to take into their own hands the training, examination and ordination of their ministers.[3] A system of examination and ordination was quickly established in connection with Wittenberg University[4] and, finally, ways had to be found to obtain curacies and titles for the ministers thus ordained, again involving a revolutionary change in the system of appointments.[5] Many of these far-reaching schemes could only be carried out with the help of the princes and city councils, and that raised the issue of the relation between Church and State.[6] In the end, practically nothing was left in the hands of the Pope and his bishops, and a completely new independent Church order emerged.

Luther did not plan far ahead with detailed schemes for the reformation of the Church. He liked to solve the problems as they came. He and his followers only refused obedience to existing things which were contrary to their conscience. But one conflict led to another and resulted in such great consequences that in the end Luther's religious preaching brought about a complete reformation of the existing Church.[7]

4. Is Luther responsible for starting the "Reformation," or is it only the necessary outcome of an historic development?

Roughly speaking, Luther's activities as a reformer began in 1517 and culminated in his great writings of 1520-3. The main trends of his doctrine were clearly fixed in his mind and already proclaimed by him in the years prior to 1517. Therefore it is obvious that Luther's reformation started earlier than the activities of the other great reformers. Zwingli's first writings advocating a reformation appeared in 1522, while Calvin was only eight years of age when Luther published his 95 Sentences. It is a

---

[1] *W.A.*, 15, 720, 12; *Tischr.*, 6,401.   [2] *W.A.*, 6, 441f.
[3] W. Friedensburg, *Nuntiaturberichte aus Deutschland 1533-1539*, Vol. I, Gotha, 1892, p. 544.
[4] P. Drews, *Die Ordination, Prüfung und Lehrverpflichtung* (*op. cit.*).
[5] e.g. *Briefw.*, Nos. 485, 496-8; *W.A.*, 12, 3ff.
[6] *Briefw.*, No. 687; *Tischr.*, 6,998.
[7] Oskar Andersen, *Superintendentembedet i den evang.-luth. Kirke og "Kirkemagten,"* in *Kirkeleksikon for Norden*, Aarhus. McKinnon, *op. cit.*, III, 11-46; 68-79; 102-37.

disputed question whether the achievements of Zwingli and Calvin would have been possible without Luther "breaking the ice." But was Luther really responsible for starting the great Reformation, or is he only the necessary link in a development, making himself the mouthpiece of thoughts which were in everybody's mind, anyhow, and which would very quickly have found some other outlet had not Luther by chance been lucky enough to be the first on the spot?

It is common to assume the existence of forerunners of the Reformation, e.g. Wycliffe and the Lollards in England, John Hus and various Bohemian reformation movements, the attempts by Gerson, Marsilius of Padua and others, to raise the authority of general Church councils above the authority of the Pope, to criticise abuses in the Church, the immorality of her priests, and the stupidity of her monks, as exposed by the Humanists. Some utterances of Luther himself may indicate that he believed Hus and the Bohemian brethren to be in the nature of spiritual predecessors of himself.[1] Therefore, some historians assume that it only needed a spark to bring about the explosion of all the accumulated gunpowder. And, voluntarily or involuntarily, Luther happened to become this spark.

This conception is violently contradicted by others, who claim that the whole Reformation, or at least the start and direction of the Reformation, was exclusively born in Luther's mind and that no one could justly claim the name of a forerunner of the Reformation. They would say that nobody had in any way paved the way for Luther's main conceptions and that the few elements in Luther that could be traced back to earlier theologians were not vital for his theological ideas and had to be completely transformed and altered by him before he could use them. Goethe passes this judgment on the Reformation:

> "Confidentially speaking, there is nothing of any interest in the whole matter apart from the character of Luther. It was this only which created any impression among people. Everything else is a complicated affair still burdening us to-day."[2]

No fair-minded judge of history could easily approve of Goethe's one-sided judgment, but many scholars would support his opinion so far as to believe that the Lutheran Reformation was primarily Luther's own personal work and that all other sixteenth-century reformers were encouraged by the beginning made by Luther. I personally am inclined to support this view, but I admit that this

---

[1] e.g. *W.A.*, 38, 75ff.; *Tischr.*, 488, 4,922, 5,485.
[2] Conversation with F. W. Riemer, August 22nd, 1806.

is such a disputed question that it would need more argument than space in this book would permit. Luther himself supports this view.[1] The reader will doubtless recognise—whatever Luther took over from others—that his main thinking is independent of his predecessors. He dares to advance in quite new ways and often he himself is afraid of the consequences.

5. *Against whom did Luther fight?*

It is wrong to believe that *all* Luther's fighting and teaching is directed solely against the Pope and his Church. The reader of his writings will be struck by the fact that Luther's struggle was directed against the Enthusiasts and Fanatics (*Schwärmer*), Anabaptists, Zwinglians, and various other religious movements which were as opposed to the Pope and the existing Church as was Luther, but in most other respects were different from him. So we have to bear in mind that Luther was fighting a two-front war, against the Pope and against enthusiastic reformation movements. And the latter was sometimes much the more vigorous. A large portion of Luther's writings is not polemical at all, but contains constructive proposals for pastoral work, music, schools and education, the German language, etc.

6. *Are Luther's theological views on the whole consistent during the time of his reformation activities?*

On this point there is no unity of judgment amongst scholars. No one will deny that there was a religious development in Luther up to the time of his becoming a reformer. But it would be interesting to know whether from then onwards he held inconsistent views during various periods of his life. It is obvious that the emphasis in Luther's writings varies according to the adversaries with whom he has to deal. Up to 1523 Luther was busy attacking and altering the existing Church. From 1524 Luther spent a good deal of his time in preventing others (if I may use the idiom) from "pouring out the baby with the bath-water." Where reforms were still necessary, he tried, nevertheless, to preserve all that was good, and he stressed the authority of the ministry against too far-reaching democratic schemes of Church government.

His trouble with Karlstadt in 1524 might have caused this change. His former friend Karlstadt became his violent enemy and

---

[1] Wycliffe and Hus, whilst attacking only more external abuses, did not attempt a real Church reformation. *Tischr.*, 22, 491, 3,795, 3,846; "*doctrinam invadere ist* [before Luther] *noch nie geschehen,*" *Tischr.*, 624.

in later years attacked Luther violently.[1] He demanded the destruction of altars and paintings in churches. In 1524 he had become Vicar at Orlamünde. Luther tried to remove him from there, pointing out to the magistrates of that city, not only that Karlstadt's doctrine and puritan practice was wrong, but also that the Elector and Wittenberg University, who as patrons had some say in the matters of that particular parish, had not been consulted by the congregation at Orlamünde. The magistrates, in defence of Karlstadt, appealed to Luther's own book of the previous year. In this book Luther had advocated "congregational" principles and proved that the Christian congregation must have complete freedom to elect its own ministers. Thus they fought Luther by quoting Luther.[2] This incident, I imagine, convinced Luther of the danger of his own too far-reaching reforms and too revolutionary books. This and the Peasants' War in the following year strongly reinforced his conservative feelings.

While such an alteration in tone and emphasis in Luther's writings can be found from 1524–5, his self-contradictions are not as great as is generally supposed. He never lost certain fundamental "revolutionary" conceptions of his earlier life, not even during his last "conservative" years, while a certain "conservative" wish not to alter more than absolutely necessary can be traced as early as in his revolutionary writings of 1520–3. In no case did he wish to cause chaos. There may be many minor contradictions in detail, but on the whole, I venture to say, that it will be easier for us to trace a certain basic consistency in Luther's writings than it will be for later generations to trace a basic consistency in Karl Barth's writings from the time of his *Letter to the Romans* up to the time of his *Letter to the Christians of Great Britain*, and yet many think that there is no fundamental change in Karl Barth.

As a general rule it is safe to say that Luther, in his later years, became more and more what we to-day call a "High Church man." He emphasises sacraments, the divine institution of the ministry, ritual, and many good usages of the early Church. He even sympathises with an episcopal Church constitution. But at the same time he became more and more aggressive against the Pope, and shortly before his death he published a violent book entitled, *Against the Papacy of Rome instituted by the Devil*, a book full of inciting expressions and acrid criticisms. And his liking for certain High Church ideas did not cause him to betray his earlier evangelical principles. For example, while on various grounds he sympathised with a kind of episcopal constitution, he

---

[1] *Tischr.*, 84, 406, 3,593, 3,724.
[2] *W.A.*, 15, 323ff.; *Tischr.*, 90.

strongly retained his earlier belief that the so-called "Apostolic Succession" through episcopal ordination is not necessary for the validity of episcopacy, ministry and sacrament. "High Anglican" and "High Lutheran" are two very different things.

II

THE DOCTRINE OF THE NATURE OF MAN[1]

1. *Human Sin*

THE spiritual leader of modern paganism in Germany in recent years, Alfred Rosenberg, once expressed the opinion that it would be easier to imagine some sort of reconciliation between National-Socialist philosophy and Catholic theology than with Protestant theology. For, as he said, Catholic theology, in accordance with Thomas Aquinas, at least admits some measure of free will, of value in man and human nature, and of natural law in general which makes it easier for Catholics to understand the National-Socialist emphasis on "natural values" like race, blood, nation, State, historic task of peoples, while Protestantism constantly preaches original sin and the necessity of repentance, and regards mankind and nature as completely corrupt and human values as without religious importance.

What does Luther really teach about the corruption of mankind?

In order to understand man's present state it is necessary to realise man in his *original* state before sin came into the world. Luther would call the original man: Adam in Paradise. He always treated the story of Adam in Paradise as an historic fact.[2] In more recent times, when critical scholarship challenged theology by denying the historic trustworthiness of the first chapters of Genesis, very many Lutherans accepted this denial in general, while others defended every word of the story, or at least tried to defend the descent of mankind from one single couple.[3] The doctrine of original sin seemed to be more easily understandable if this were accepted. Such Lutherans tried to show that mankind—in spite of its variety of races—had so much in common everywhere as to make its descent from *one* couple very probable. They also endeavoured to prove the inconsistency of science which, on one hand, tried to show that the various races could not be explained if all men came from one couple, while, on the

[1] For the whole chapter, cf. J. Köstlin, *Luthers Theologie in ihrer geschichtlichen Entwicklung und ihrem inneren Zusammenhange*, Stuttgart, 1901, Vol. II, 110–29; Elert, *op. cit.*, I, 15–52.

[2] e.g. *Tischr.*, 5,505; Luther thinks that the lapse took place at about 2 p.m.

[3] Luther's attitude to the historical trustworthiness of the Bible, see below, pp. 118ff.

other hand, trying to prove the descent of man from the monkey.[1] Other Lutherans preferred to treat the story of Adam as symbolising "the original man" or "mankind in its original state." No wonder that modern racial theories, denying the biological unity of mankind and teaching the permanent existence of superior and inferior races, raise many problems for orthodox Lutheran theology. They ought to be unacceptable to an orthodox Lutheran, but, as quite a number of so-called Lutherans on the Continent accepted them, they provoked a violent conflict within the German Lutheran Church.

Yet most of the more liberal Lutherans would agree that their conviction that Paradise is not an historic fact, does not mean that we are without sin. They would say that the deeper content of the story is not necessarily dependent on its historical correctness.[2]

Luther does not describe the state of man in Paradise in all details. He did not write a book entitled *The Theology of Adam*, as happened in later Lutheranism. And yet he says quite a lot on this subject.[3] Adam's intellect was stronger than ours; his body better, his eyes and ears sharper. He did work in the garden, but without pain and sweat. Nature was pleasanter than nowadays; animals not dangerous; the land without thorns and thistles, the sun brighter. Love of God and faith in God belonged to Adam's nature in the same way as the reception of light belongs to the nature of eyes. In his married life with Eve, sexual intercourse took place, not in uncontrolled and wild desire as nowadays when our flesh became "leprous" by sin, but in highest moderation, as a kind of worship of God. To all outward appearance, life was much the same before the lapse as after: there was work and there was marriage in Paradise. No ascetic tendencies can be traced in Luther in this respect. What mattered was the attitude to things, the spirit and the feelings causing and accompanying the acts of man. In Paradise Adam did all things in obedience to God, in confidence in God, not in revolt against Him. And the end awaiting Adam and Eve was not death, but a life of permanent youth preserved through eating of the Tree of Life and finally transformation into higher, spiritual, angel-like life.[4]

The Fall of man destroyed all this and Luther is convinced that this lapse of the original man has become the cause of all our miseries. Sin once accepted by Adam became a constant power in man.

[1] cf. K. v. Hase, *Hutterus Redivivus*, Leipzig, 12th ed. 1883, § 79, pp. 160f.
[2] e.g. R. Niebuhr, *An Interpretation of Christian Ethics*, London, 1936, pp. 23ff.
[3] e.g. in his lectures on Genesis (*W.A.*, 42) and in sermons (see Köstlin, *ibid.*).
[4] Köstlin, *op. cit.*, II, 112ff.; *Tischr.*, 4,309.

What was the chief wrong in Adam and Eve eating the fruit? The mistrust of God's word and goodwill to man which had imposed the prohibition. Such unbelief is the source of all sin. And unbelief is essentially Luther's idea of sin in general.[1] The very question, Why has God forbidden us to eat from that tree? reveals the beginning of this unbelief and already contains the fulness and depth of sin.

There were great disputes in Protestant theology about the question of whether Adam and Eve had the power to resist the temptation if they wished, whether there had been any chance of their living without sin. Some theologians asserted that Adam and Eve had free will to choose the right path, and that of their own free will they made the wrong decision.[2] Others—especially strict Calvinists—maintained that the Fall of man had been decided by divine decree before ever man was created.[3] In Milton's *Paradise Lost*, God says about Adam and Eve:

" . . . *They themselves decreed*
Their own revolt, not I. If I foreknew
Foreknowledge had no influence on their fault,
Which had no less proved certain unforeknown.

. . . .

I formed them free and free they must remain
Till they enthral themselves: I else must change
Their nature and revoke the high decree
Unchangeable, eternal, which ordained
Their freedom. They themselves ordained their fall.
The first sort by their own suggestion fell,
Self tempted, self depraved: Man falls, deceived
By the other first. . . ."

Luther does not speak about these things in the same detailed manner as Milton does. But a word of his suggesting that Adam, had he been tempted before Eve, would probably have conquered,[4] implies that man had the possibility and even the task of conquering the temptation. But as he succumbed, he lost this gift of free will and could no longer live without sinning. Luther does not solve the riddle why the almighty and good God could not prevent

---

[1] W.A., 5, 50, 8; 16, 320; 16, 417, 8ff.; 39, I, 345, 26; 42, 133, 9; 43, 302, 10; *Bekenntnisschriften*, 433ff. (*Schmalk. Art.*, 3, 2).

[2] Infra-lapsarian predestination, i.e. the lapse itself was not predestined by God.

[3] Supra-lapsarian predestination.   [4] Köstlin, *op. cit.*, II, 117.

the Devil from bringing evil to the world. Luther rejects the question why God allowed Satan to tempt Adam as a typical question of human impertinence. What we have to learn from the story is that our own free will is no good if left to itself and not governed by God's spirit.

In Luther's eyes sin is mainly our wrong attitude towards God. The Augsburg Confession summarises this conception well when describing man after the fall: *sine metu Dei, sine fiducia erga Deum et cum concupiscentia* (without fear of God, without confidence in God and with evil lust).[1] But the word *concupiscentia* means much more than a sinful attitude in the sexual sphere. In contrast to the general ideas of his time, Luther makes it clear that evil lust is not only and not even predominantly a wild sexual desire. The expression "Sins of the flesh" does not only describe the lack of chastity, the "low and small desires" as Luther calls them, but also the "high and evil desires," meaning the ambitions of human knowledge and reason, the corruption both of body and soul, wrath and aggressive will, and the pride of human intellect.[2] *Concupiscentia* means our whole uncontrolled selfish life ruled by demons.

Thus sin spoilt even the good things in the world. Our attitude to God and to our own desires spoils the good institution of matrimony. It is entirely wrong, in Luther's view, to try to escape sinful things by celibacy and life as a monk. One cannot avoid the sins of the world by forsaking the world. Luther's outspoken condemnation of the immorality of the monasteries and convents of his time is not born primarily of moral indignation, but he wants to show that sin and a sinful attitude cannot be avoided by denying a normal life. Sin will become much stronger and the consequences more disastrous when we try to flee from a normal life. Thus the monastery is not different from the "world" and may be a form of extreme selfishness.[3] Neither civil enterprise nor secular work nor marriage are bad and sinful in themselves, but *we* are bad and sinful.

This applies to *all* men who are not saved by Christ. It also applies to good pagans. Certainly Luther is not blind to what he calls "*egregia opera, honestissima facta*" (marvellous achievements, most honourable acts) as shown by great and decent pagan men—he quotes Socrates, Themistocles, Cicero and others.[4] But, while he does not stress the idea that "the heathens' virtues are but splendid vices," he makes it quite clear that good pagans are in

[1] Augsburg Conf., Art. II.   [2] Köstlin, *op. cit.*, II, 119f.
[3] cf. D. Bonhoeffer, *Nachfolge*, München, 1937, p. 5.
[4] *Tischr.*, 155, 3,608d, 3,925, 5,012, 5,440.

no way free from original sin and that their good deeds cannot be separated from the sinful roots of their life.¹

Luther takes sin terribly seriously. Humanly speaking, there do exist more or less decent people, but this must not make us blind to the reality that before God *all* people are sinners, that even our so-called good deeds are polluted by complacency or the selfish attitude accompanying them. None of us can fulfil Christ's commandment to love God with all our heart and our neighbour as ourselves. Therefore, "all our own works are in vain even in the best life."²

This is the terrible law of "original sin." The sin of the first man and woman has affected all mankind. There is no individual responsibility in the sense that the second or third man had their own chance of avoiding sin. Once sin ruled in human flesh, it passed from generation to generation.³

2. *The origin of the soul*

The doctrine of original sin makes Luther prefer the so-called "traducianistic" theory of the origin of the human soul.

There are three main theories about the origin of the soul. First, there is the "pre-existence" theory asserting that our soul existed long before our present life and was put into our body, living there like the bird in its cage, up to the day of our death when the soul can fly away. This idea is mainly associated with philosophical schools connected with the name of Plato and influenced Christianity through Neo-Platonism.⁴

The second theory, as favoured by the Catholic Church, is called "creatianism." God creates a new soul for every child that is born. Luther dislikes this idea that a soul, newly created by God in purity, should be connected with sinful human flesh and thus polluted.⁵ He holds the third theory, i.e. that not only the sinful human flesh and body is an inheritance of our forefathers, but that even the soul comes from our parents in the same way as our body does. This "traducianistic" theory is supported by the fact that not only physical but also spiritual qualities of the parents are inherited by the children. It is vital for Luther that men as natural human beings inherit the sinful character of former generations, but he does not like hair-splitting discussions about the

---

¹ Köstlin, *op. cit.*, I, 10; II, 123.
² Hymn: "*Aus tiefer Not schrei ich zu dir,*" verse 2, *Deutsches Evangelisches Gesangbuch*, No. 140.
³ On the whole subject, cf. Elert, *op. cit.*, I, 25ff.
⁴ Apparently Luther sympathised with this conception in his early years. *W.A.*, 4, 342.
⁵ *Tischr.*, 5,230.

way in which this happens. He says that his own theory was not binding for the Church, and that different theories on this point might be tolerated.¹

3. *Free will*

The eagerly disputed question of "free will" eventually brought about the rupture between Luther and Erasmus in 1525. What was Luther's opinion?²

Man, he held, had free will as regards a number of external occupations and decisions, whether he wants to trade, to speak, to marry, to walk or not. Luther describes these things as *naturalia, res rationi subjectae, res civiles*, governing cows, horses, money and possessions. Even in his outspoken book against Erasmus he admits some amount of free will with regard to these *res inferiores*, as he calls them. This free will does not only enable us to walk for secular purposes, but also to walk to church or to read religious books.

But man is unable to decide of his own free will, to grasp and believe the things which he hears at church; he cannot accept salvation by Christ as a consequence of a decision of his own. To make this clear, not in Luther's words but my own, let us take human love as an example: I cannot say: "from to-morrow I will love this or that person." I only can meet that person, speak to him, try to understand him and then suddenly or in the course of time I may feel: "I like, or even I love this person." But it is likewise quite possible that as a result of my knowing him I dislike him in the end.

Nobody can decide: from to-morrow I will believe in Christ. I only can go to church, hear about Christ, think about Him, read Christian books, and in the course of time the Holy Spirit may create faith in me and I feel: now I can believe. But it is quite possible that I do not believe in spite of all my efforts. This last decision of faith depends not on my effort but on God's calling me (Rom. ix. 16).

This is one of the reasons for the distrust felt in Lutheran theology of those ceremonies which seem to suggest that the Holy Spirit can be transferred by the will of man through episcopal consecration or confirmation. The attempt to prove such ideas from Acts viii. 14-17 (the story in which the Holy Spirit is apparently transferred by the apostolic laying-on of hands) fails; for

¹ P. Althaus, *Die letzten Dinge*, Gütersloh, 1933, pp. 88ff., 155ff.; cf. Köstlin, *op. cit.*, II, 120ff.
² On the whole subject, cf. Luther's book against Erasmus, *De servo arbitrio*, *W.A.*, 18, 600-787; cf. McKinnon, *op. cit.*, III, 251-73.

other examples show that God can give the Holy Spirit without such ceremony whenever He wishes, even *before* baptism, as in the case of Cornelius and his company (Acts x).

A modern Anglican describes Luther's conception in a rather outspoken way:

"But an unconverted man, in his 'fallen' state, is limited to co-operation in what are called 'external things'—that is to say, he can decide whether or not to attend a meeting at which the word of God is being preached. Once he has moved his legs so as to place his body within earshot of the preacher, he has no part to play in whatever internal change may be wrought in him. If, however, he does not turn his feet into the required direction, it follows that he does not hear the preaching and receive the illumination of the Spirit, in which case he remains outside the sphere of God's mercy, and his condemnation is just because he despises the medium of the Spirit's working and does not wish to hear the word of God."[1]

Some contemporaries of the Reformation believed that one question was not clearly decided by Luther: if God convinces me through His word and offers me faith and causes me to feel called by God—can I resist? Is grace irresistible? Is it a general rule that man can be converted against his own will as it seems to be in the example of St. Paul's conversion outside Damascus?

The last Lutheran Confession, the *Formula Concordiae*, tries to decide this question which had caused controversies after Luther's lifetime.[2] It says that man is at least able to say "No" if God calls him, he is for a short moment given back his free will to decide whether he wants to resist or not. We might perhaps say: it is not in our power whether the sun shines or not, but we may open the window when it shines, or, on the other hand, we may draw the curtain and shut it out. This interpretation could be encouraged by the word of Christ to the citizens of Jerusalem: "how often would I have gathered thy children together, even as a hen gathereth her chickens under her wings, and *ye would not*" (Matt. xxiii. 37; cf. Acts vii. 51).[3]

---

[1] L. Hodgson, *The Grace of God in Faith and Philosophy*, Bishop Paddock Lectures, 1936, p. 43.
[2] *Formula of Concord*, Epit. XI, II; Sol. Dec., II, 73ff.; XI, 41f., 78 (*Bekenntnisschriften*, pp. 819, 902ff., 1,076, 1,085f.); cf. *Popular Symbolics*, ed. by Th. Engelden, W. Arndt, Th. Graebner, F. E. Mayer, St. Louis, 1934, p. 58 ("resistible grace").
[3] "*Wir unterliegen, solange wir wollend sind, einem inneren Gesetz der Schwere, und Luther gebraucht darum den Ausdruck, dass wir fallen, wie auch, dass wir wohl nach unten, aber nicht nach oben frei sind.*" Ricarda Huch, *Luthers Glaube*, Leipzig, 1917, pp. 10f.

There are passages in the Bible claiming that "God willeth that all men should be saved and come to the knowledge of the truth";[1] on the other hand there are utterances showing that, in spite of this will of the Almighty God, many people are lost for ever.[2] Luther and the Lutherans after him did not try to reconcile apparent contradictions in the Bible. They take both sides as they stand without trying to smooth over the cleavage.[3] This principle applied to our present problem causes Luther to make a distinction: there is God as revealed to us, the *"Deus revelatus,"* God who wants to invite all mankind to be saved. But there is a riddle in God, the *"Deus absconditus"* (hidden God), who causes, or at least permits, many human beings to be lost for ever. It is the preacher's task to preach the *Deus revelatus* and to offer salvation to everyone; it is not his task to preach the *Deus absconditus*. We cannot understand the latter, but we know He exists.[4]

4. The Devil

Another example of Luther's tendency to stress contradicting Biblical statements without trying to explain them or to smooth them over is his approach to the question of the Devil. The Devil is God's enemy, and God is almighty. But the Almighty God does not try to destroy His enemy and his pernicious activities. And yet God is not responsible for the evil caused by the activities of the Devil. But there are not two Gods. Sometimes it sounds in Luther's sermons and hymns as if the world were a battlefield between two equal powers, a good God and an evil god called Devil, but then he strongly emphasises the fact that God is almighty and the Devil, in spite of being God's enemy, is somehow always "God's Devil." Luther does not try to bridge the gulf.[5]

[1] 1 Tim. ii. 4.

[2] e.g. Matt. xiii. 11-15.

[3] cf. the passages on the difference between Lutheran, Calvinistic and Arminian Churches in *Popular Symbolics* (*op. cit.*), pp. 223ff.

[4] Elert, *op. cit.*, I, pp. 18ff., 103ff.

[5] It would be of interest, though it would lead too far here, to go into the question of Luther's teaching about the Devil and good and evil spirits. He believes, not only in the one Devil, but also in demons and angels. His belief in good and evil spirits plays a greater part in Luther's teaching than present-day theology cares to emphasise. He also believes in spooks (*Poltergeister*) (*Tischr.*, 3,814, 6,816), but he is doubtful whether these phenomena are souls of dead people (*W.A.*, 30, II, 385; *Tischr.*, 3,695) or whether they are demons who are connected with the Devil. I can only refer students of this question to Köstlin, *op. cit.*, II, 102ff. On his teaching about the Devil as a great power opposed to God, cf. e.g. *Tischr.*, 4,989; K. Heim, *Jesus der Weltvollender*, Berlin, 1937; G. Aulén, *Christus Victor*, London, S.P.C.K., 1931 (the Swedish original: *Den Kristna Forsoningstanken*, Stockholm, 1930).

5. Predestination[1]

The same principles apply to the question of predestination. Luther knows—as Milton did—the difference between God's foreknowledge of things and His decree ordering in advance men's salvation—between *praescientia* and *praedestinatio*. But he thinks for all practical purposes there is no great difference between them. If God knows beforehand that I will be lost, this fact is already decided.

And yet it is not the task of the preacher to proclaim that God may have decided the ultimate judgment on me. These attempts to explore the inexplorable will of God must be discouraged by all means.[2] Man ought to keep to the Saviour's word, John xxi. 22. It is the task of the preacher to offer me salvation. If I hear the word, if it impresses me, I should feel I am invited to the Kingdom of God, I am offered the truth and I should feel confident that I am saved, that God wants me to be a believer. In this right understanding the doctrine of predestination is not a terrifying but a consoling doctrine. But on the other hand, I should not rely on a false sense of security and should always remember that God is the ultimate judge.

6. Ordinances of creation

Some recent German theologians, anxious to secure a compromise with National-Socialist ideology, claimed that it was not contrary to Christianity to worship one's own nation and race and to adore a totalitarian State, because God had created nations and States. For them nation, race, blood and State were "ordinances of creation" (*Schöpfungsordnungen*).[3] Opposing theologians, however, claimed that these things were not part of God's original creation and that the Bible had every reason to distinguish between the original divine ordinances which were valid in Paradise (like marriage), and those ordinances which were introduced by God after Adam's fall and the murder of Cain in order to avoid complete chaos. These latter ordinances were called "ordinances of preservation" (*Erhaltungsordnungen*). There were no States or police necessary in Paradise. A modern English Nonconformist rightly summarises the Lutheran doctrine in these words:

---

[1] On the whole subject, cf. Elert, *op. cit.*, I, 103–11; *W.A.*, 18, 600–787; Köstlin, *op. cit.*, II, 74ff. *Popular Symbolics, op. cit.*, pp. 74f., 124–80.

[2] *Tischr.*, 502, 3,655b, 5,070.

[3] cf. P. Althaus, *Grundriss der Ethik*, Erlangen, 1931 (sic), pp. 94–112.

"The task of the State, therefore, is not to set up Paradise on earth, but to prevent earth becoming hell. The State, unlike marriage, is not part of the Creator's original intention for mankind; it is vouchsafed by divine mercy as a result of the fall and in restraint of sin. Were it not for the coercive power of the State, human life would degenerate into pure anarchy. . . . The basis . . . of the State is force. . . . The State may be better or worse, but, whatever it is, it must be accepted as God's merciful gift in restraint of anarchy. . . ."[1]

[1] N. Micklem, *The Theology of Politics*, Oxford, 1941, pp. 45f.; cf. *Tischr.*, 162.

III

THE DOCTRINE OF SALVATION[1]

WHAT is man's way out of the state of utter corruption and sinfulness? There is no doubt, for Luther, that the way is called "Jesus Christ." What does Luther teach about Jesus Christ?

1. *Person of Christ*

Luther would in no way accept unitarian ideas. For him no one is a Christian who does not believe that Christ at the same time is true man and true God. He is the second Person of the Trinity. Luther accepts the trinitarian early Church creeds, not only as a matter of tradition, but out of deep conviction.[2] The long Athanasian Creed, describing in detail the traditional Church doctrine of the Trinity, was especially liked by Luther.[3] So was the second article of the Creed, and his explanation of this article in the Shorter Catechism (where he explains the Apostolio Creed) is supposed by many people to be the most beautiful sentence in the German language. Rome did not accuse Luther of heresy in questions of Christology and Trinity; and Luther himself is rightly or wrongly convinced that in this sphere he holds the traditional doctrine.

There is, however, one point of special interest in Luther's doctrine on Christ. It became known by the name *communicatio idiomatum*. The *idiomata*, i.e. the attributes by which the human and the divine nature can be described, are to some degree interchangeable in the person of Christ. For instance, God can be everywhere. A man can only be at one place at a time. In so far as Christ is God, He can be everywhere. But even the human nature of Christ, even His body as seen and touched by the disciples after the Resurrection, shares the quality of the divine nature and can now be everywhere. There are passages suggesting that Luther ascribes this *communicatio idiomatum* and omnipresence of the body of Christ even to the time before His

---

[1] On the whole subject, cf. Köstlin, *op. cit.*, II, 129–72; Elert, *op. cit.*, I, 195–223; Holl, *op. cit.*, pp. 111–54; *Popular Symbolics*, *op. cit.*, pp. 42–100.

[2] *W.A.*, 26, 500, 10.

[3] cf. Kattenbusch, *Luthers Stellung zu den oekumenischen Symbolen*, Giessen, 1883; Elert, *op. cit.*, I, 180ff.

Resurrection and Ascension. The Ascension in this case was only the wonderful revelation of a mystery "kept secret" by Christ up to then. Other passages, however, seem to suggest that the full exaltation of the human nature of Christ took place only at the Ascension. The idea that Christ had to "keep secret" certain divine qualities during His earthly life later on brought about disputes among Lutherans whether this was a *krypsis* (keeping secret) or a *kenosis* (emptying himself) (Phil. ii. 7).[1]

This doctrine on the omnipresence of both natures of Christ makes Luther fight against the mediæval idea that heaven is a place somewhere above. Christ is sitting on the right hand of God, the Father Almighty. But it is obvious that God has no right hand in a bodily sense. God is everywhere. He fills heaven and earth. We act with our right hand. Everywhere where God is active there is His right hand—*dextera Dei est ubique*—and if Christ sits on the right hand of God, also He is everywhere, and not only His divine nature, but also His transformed, resurrected body.[2]

Three facts in connection with these thoughts deserve emphasis:

(1) It is vital for Luther that Christ's body can now be everywhere, for in this way only it seems possible for him that Christ's flesh and blood can really be present at the same time in all those many thousand churches where the Lord's Supper is celebrated. For Luther believes in the Real Presence of Christ's flesh and blood in Holy Communion.

(2) Many Lutherans thought in later years that these principles were formally rejected by the so-called "black rubric" and Article XXVIII of the Anglican Prayer Book. I know that it is possible to interpret in different ways the sentence of the "black rubric": "The natural body and blood of our Saviour Christ are in heaven and not here: it being against the truth of Christ's natural body to be at one time in more places than one." The Lutherans felt—rightly or wrongly—this rubric to be directed, not only against transubstantiation, but also against Luther's doctrine. This is one of the main reasons why many Lutherans refused intercommunion with the Church of England. A dispute of this kind took place in the time of Queen Anne and the Lutheran Prince Consort, Prince George of Denmark. As far as I know, the obstacle at that time was not the question of episcopacy or reconfirmation, but the Lutherans took offence at this rubric and some calvinistic conceptions in the Thirty-nine Articles, and

---

[1] Karl v. Hase, *Hutterus redivivus* (*op. cit.*), pp. 217–25, esp. 218, note 3.

[2] e.g. *W.A.*, 26, 314–18; cf. Formula of Concord (*Bekenntnisschriften*, p. 1,006f.); *Tischr.*, III.

therefore some of them did not want to allow intercommunion with this "calvinistic" Church of England.[1]

(3) Luther was no scholar of science, and still rather mediæval in his conception of the structure of the world. He did not like Copernicus and his new idea that the earth revolved round the sun. And yet this doctrine of Luther's, of heaven being everywhere, caused many Lutherans to tolerate the new ideas of Copernicus. They were no longer interested in heaven being a local place somewhere above. Copernicus could publish his books in Lutheran countries.

2. *Work of Christ*[2]

There are people who claim that the Cross has an educational value only, revealing God's attitude towards man and setting a glorious example, but that the Cross does not alter facts, does not bring about a change of attitude in God, transforming God's wrath into God's grace.

Luther's opinion on this point is quite definite. For him the Cross means the real act, a real change in God's attitude, a transformation of God's wrath into God's grace—it means the fight between life and death.[3] It is not only an instructive revelation, but something *happens* on the Cross.

While this fundamental issue is clear, the details are much less clear. What actually does happen on the Cross? Again Luther dislikes the speculations of human reason. It is enough simply and modestly to accept whatever thoughts the Bible offers us.

One may say that Luther's conceptions concerning the work of Christ, concerning the salvation brought about by Him, follow two main lines:[4]

(1) One line of thought is mainly related to the old ideas of "satisfaction." God's holiness and justice are so great that He cannot overlook the fact of human guilt and disobedience against Himself. Punishment is inevitable. Christ bears our punishment, takes our sins upon Himself, is banned and condemned by God in our place. This doctrine of Atonement is not developed by Luther once more into a great system as previously by Anselm

---

[1] cf. J. Rieger, "The British Crown and the German Churches in England," in *And Other Pastors of Thy Flock*, ed. by F. Hildebrandt, Cambridge, 1942, pp. 104f.

[2] See Elert, *op. cit.*, I, 93–110.

[3] "*Es war ein wunderlich Krieg/ da Tod und Leben rungen/ Das Leben behielt den Sieg/ es hat den Tod verschlungen/ Die Schrift hat verkündet das/ wie ein Tod den andern frass/ Ein Spott der Tod ist worden.*" *Dtsch. Ev. Gesangbuch*, No. 57, verse 4.

[4] See above, p. 41, note 5.

and the scholastics. But many of Luther's utterances refer to Christ as suffering for us in order to give satisfaction for us to God. This makes Luther convinced of the necessity that Christ should *feel* forsaken and condemned by God on the Cross; that He should *say* "My God, my God, why hast thou forsaken me?" But, further, Luther thinks that Christ really *was* forsaken and condemned by God at this moment, that "Him who knew no sin He made to be sin on our behalf" (2 Cor. v. 21) because only in this way could He suffer those depths of despair which we deserve to suffer "that we might become the righteousness of God in Him."

(2) The other line of thought followed by Luther clearly interprets the Cross and Resurrection of Christ as a fight between God and the Devil. This idea is strongly emphasised in sermons and hymns. Christ's death and Resurrection wins the victory over the evil powers, "sin, death and devil," as Luther likes to summarise them. Modern Lutheran scholars, like Professor Karl Heim and the Swedish Bishop Gustaf Aulén, do not only think that this is Luther's main conception of the work of Christ, but that this represents the best interpretation of the doctrine of the Bible and the early Church. The deep tension underlying the story of Christ's Passion indicates that a tremendous fight takes place between God and the Devil. God conquers the Devil by allowing Himself in Christ to be destroyed by devilish power without resisting the Devil, in spite of the fact that He could easily have done so. This was such an enormous task that only in this way can we understand the proper meaning of Christ's temptation to evade this task and His agony in the Garden of Gethsemane and that His sweat became, as it were, great drops of blood falling down upon the ground.[1]

Luther thinks that the Catholics under-estimate the importance of the Atonement and narrow the scope of Christ's work because they allow human merits and good works to share in the achievement bringing about our salvation. For Luther the work of Christ is the only factor in our salvation, while for the Catholics, as, rightly or wrongly, Luther sees them, Christ's work only covers one part of the factors necessary for salvation. The remaining part is left to human efforts.

3. *Justification*[2]

That brings us to the question of justification. Here we are faced with two alternatives: (1) Does God declare a man to be

[1] Heim, *op. cit.*, pp. 116-27.
[2] For the following, see Köstlin, *op. cit.*, II, 173-219; Holl, *op. cit.*, iii-154; Elert, *op. cit.*, I, 123-54.

justified on the ground of Christ's work? Or (2) does the work of Christ cause a man to improve in such a degree that God can justly recognise him as justified on the ground of his improved quality?

To make it clear by an analogy: (1) Does the work of Christ pay man's debts? Or (2) does it only give to man the training and qualities enabling him to earn sufficient money to pay his debts by himself?

The first conception is called "forensic." This indicates that the justification is seen as a procedure before a court of law (*forum*), in front of a tribunal. Man has not improved yet, but God imputes Christ's merits to him. By a decision of the tribunal, man is declared to be justified on the ground of Christ's merits. Melanchthon, Luther's friend, held this view.

The other conception would mean that the work of Christ can so improve a man as to enable him to become really good in the eyes of God. In this case the work of Christ would only help a man to earn salvation through his own merits. This extreme conception was, of course, never held by Lutherans. But there was a theological school inside Lutheranism, headed by one called A. Osiander, attempting a compromise between the two alternatives. This caused a major conflict soon after Luther's death.

Osiander said that faith in Christ starts the process of improvement in man, and, while no man—not even the Christian believer—will become perfect on earth, God sees the beginning of improvement and knows that one day this beginning will lead on to final perfection in heaven. God accepts man, not only on the merit of Christ, but also on the ground of this process started in man through Christ, a process which *sub specie aeternitatis* makes man really just, and justified in the eyes of God. Melanchthon admitted that the believing Christian had to improve after being saved by God's grace alone, but he did not think that this improvement played any part in his justification and his being accepted by God.

Both theologians probably thought they represented Luther's opinion.[1] Luther was no longer alive, but, judged in the light of his writings, both Melanchthon and Osiander overstated their point. Luther would have admitted that the bringing forth of fruits, the start of a new life in man, is necessarily connected with man's salvation. When God accepts the sinner and thus establishes a deep communion between Himself and the sinner, He has the intention of really improving and healing the sinner whom He has accepted. Luther liked to explain his thought with the example of the Good Samaritan, who accepted and helped the

[1] The following argument is fully explained by Holl, *op. cit.*, pp. 119–22.

THE DOCTRINE OF SALVATION

half-dead man, he not being able to contribute to his own salvation and healing. The Good Samaritan wishes to cure him. Thus *"Deus illum* [the sinner] *assumpsit perficiendum et sanandum sicut Samaritanus semivivum relictum."*[1] This perfection, however, is impossible on this earth. No living being can ever become just in the eyes of God. Only through death and the Last Judgment can we acquire that state of perfection *"donec perfecti sanentur quod fit in morte."*[2] "We are following Christ, accepting redemption and forgiveness of sins from Him until we too become perfectly holy and need no more forgiveness."[3] "... *donec vere et prorsus purgatur (peccatum), hoc fiet in fovea sepulchri donec perveniamus ad vitam aeternam, quod fit in ultimo iudicio."*[4]

And yet Luther would on the whole support Melanchthon's line of argument. Not the improvement in man, but the work of Christ, causes God to accept man as justified. Justification and improvement are both only the consequence of Christ's work. We could say in our own words: The light of the Christian is like the light of the moon, i.e. only reflected light, entirely the work of the sun.

4. *Faith*

But how can a man be related to the work of Christ? Luther would say: By faith only. None have the benefit of Christ's work but the faithful believers. It is, however, very easy to misunderstand the meaning of the word "faith" in Luther's writings. The German word *Glaube* can either be translated as "faith" or "belief," and Luther actually uses the word to include both meanings.

Luther's term *Glaube* covers both the belief in historical facts and the personal relationship of man to God. Protestant theology uses two expressions to distinguish between both: *fides historica* and *fides salvifica*—the historical and the saving faith—or two other expressions: *fides* quae *creditur* and *fides* qua *creditur*, i.e. the faith comprising the things that are believed, and the faith by which we believe.[5]

5. *Historic faith (belief)*

It cannot be denied that Luther's conception of *Glaube* covers the sphere of certain historical facts that must be accepted as

---

[1] *W.A.*, 2, 332, 20.   [2] *W.A.*, 2, 73, 31.   [3] *W.A.*, 50, 642, 36.

[4] *Disput.*, p. 61; Drews, quoted from Holl, *op. cit.*, p. 122, note 3.

[5] L. Ihmels, "*Fides qua creditur und Fides quae creditur*," in "*Credo Ecclesiam*," *Festgabe für W. Zoellner* ed. H. P. Ehrenberg, Gütersloh, 1930, pp. 329ff.

D

true. His estimation of the Athanasian Creed, which demands belief in all the details of trinitarian doctrine as necessary for salvation, is a proof of this; similarly, his emphasis on pure doctrine and his liking for the definition of Heb. xi. 1: "Now faith is the substance of things hoped for, the evidence of things not seen."

It is open to discussion how far Luther really demanded the intellectual grasp by laymen of all theological conceptions in his doctrine. Can he really expect pious, religious old women to get all distinctions of the Augsburg Confession or the Athanasian Creed clearly into their heads?[1] But the *substance* of his doctrine must be understood by everybody in his Church and a kind of basic belief accepted. As for the rest, some Lutheran theologians think that one may distinguish between *fides explicita* and *fides implicita*, while not everybody could be expected to be able to *explain* intellectually all details of theological doctrine, this whole doctrine was supposed to be *implied* in the faith of simple believers.[2]

Luther, at least, demands a kind of basic theological training for all normal Christians. His Shorter Catechism contains that minimum of Christian knowledge demanded from everybody who wants to be a full member of the Church. This Catechism contains quite a large amount of "theology" in perfectly "untheological" language. The substance of Christian doctrine is expressed in a way understandable to the common man. This Catechism was published in 1529. But, some years earlier, in 1523, Luther surprised his congregation by the announcement that in future nobody would be admitted to the Lord's Table who was not previously examined and had shown a certain amount of basic knowledge of the meaning of the Sacrament. This examination soon took the place of what previously had been sacramental Confirmation.[3] Luther abolished sacramental Confirmation, ordaining that instruction and examination of the young Christians should take its place. Later on (mainly in the eighteenth century) an act of Confirmation was re-introduced in most Lutheran Churches. But its validity depends in no way on episcopal laying on of hands. In all Lutheran Churches the ordinary parish priest confirms. The validity of Confirmation depends on a thorough instruction lasting one or two years, some kind of private or public examination and a public confession of faith by the candidates

---

[1] *Vera theologia est practica, non speculativa*, Tischr., 153; cf. 228 and 644.

[2] This distinction criticised by L. Ihmels, *ibid.*, pp. 330ff.

[3] *W.A.*, 12, 476ff., esp. p. 478, 16; 479, 14; Tischr., 3,875; cf. *W.A.*, 12, 215f., 26, 220, 7; 232, 26; *Briefw.*, No. 678 (October 1523); *Bekenntnisschriften* p. 503, 11 (Preface to Shorter Catechism); p. 554 (Preface to Longer Catechism); p. 708 (Longer Catechism, on the Sacrament of the Altar).

to be confirmed. Upon this public confession before the congregation follows the declaration of the minister that these Christians, being baptised as infants,[1] now knowing the basic facts of their belief, are recognised as full, responsible members of the Church. One could call this act an ecclesiastical "coming of age." It is a matter of course that prayers are offered for these young Christians, and in most Lutheran Churches the minister or ministers present follow the Biblical example of the laying on of hands. But this ceremony is only an old Biblical custom, not in any way necessary to the act of Confirmation. The Swedish priests omit the laying on of hands at Confirmation, and if hymns are sung and prayers offered asking the Holy Spirit to guide the candidates, it is not meant to be an act of transferring the Holy Spirit, but only an act of prayer.

The differences between Anglican and Lutheran Confirmation are profound. Lutherans would not accept episcopal Confirmation in itself as either valid or invalid, but if an episcopally confirmed person would wish to join the Lutheran Church, they would make sure whether he has learnt enough and holds the right belief. The difference became clear in the negotiations on intercommunion between the Church of England and the Church of Sweden: the Anglicans wanted the Swedish priests to lay on hands at the Confirmation, while the Swedish bishops wanted the Church of England to enforce a longer and better instruction in connection with Confirmation.[2]

6. *Saving faith*

While Luther thus demands a certain acceptance of the "pure doctrine" and "historic faith," he thinks it is not sufficient to recognise the facts of Christian doctrine in an intellectual way only; it is not enough to acknowledge the creeds to be correct representations of facts. We have to apply all these facts to *ourselves*. *I* have to believe that *my* sins are forgiven, that Christ has died for *me*; that *I* will experience the resurrection of the body and the life everlasting; and, if I begin to believe these facts to be valid for *me*, my faith becomes more than a recognition of historic

---

[1] Adults are baptised in the Lutheran Church after thorough preparation; therefore they need no special Confirmation, but adult baptism carries with it all the privileges of Confirmation. A child which inherits a sum of money is entitled to the benefit of this money, but cannot administer it himself. Only when the child comes of age has he the right to administer the money. An adult who inherits a sum of money can administer it immediately. Thus baptised children have already the benefit of the privileges granted to them in baptism, but only through Confirmation they acquire the rights and duties of full Church membership.

[2] G. K. A. Bell, *Documents on Christian Unity*, 1920-4, Oxford Univ. Press, 1924, pp. 193f.

facts and the intellectual grasping of Christain doctrines. My faith becomes a living power relating me to Christ, changing my whole personal life. Luther highly praises this kind of faith everywhere in his writings and preaching. If a man gets this faith he feels as if he had been dead before and now becomes living and breathing. Therefore this faith is an active thing; the main power in our lives.

This faith brings about a close unity between us and Christ, who by faith becomes our redeemer and brother alike. The believer becomes *ein Kuche* (one cake) with Christ. In this connection, Luther does use words like those of mediæval mystics praising our mystical union with Christ. During the period of Lutheran orthodoxy, soon after Luther's lifetime, the theologians even clearly spoke of *unio mystica*, and extended this relation of the believer in Christ to the whole Trinity. But it is noteworthy that Luther never claims that the believer becomes "one cake" with the Trinitarian God. He seems to feel that this way of speaking would make God too familiar to us and reduce the distance between God and man to an extent which could not be permitted. Therefore Luther constantly emphasises that this whole living connection with God, through faith, is the gift of God and that we are unworthy of it. And yet this faith lifts us up into the sphere of God and bestows on us the supreme feeling of sharing with Christ His power, triumph and glory.[1]

The two sides of the faith: (*a*) the belief in historic facts, and (*b*) the living relation to God, reveal the principle under which Luther connects historic and divine things. This principle is based on the two natures in Christ, the human and the divine nature. One cannot have one nature in Christ only; one cannot merge the two natures into one. And yet there is an intimate and close connection between both.

7. *Finitum capax infiniti*[2]

This same principle can be traced in Luther's theology very frequently. Divine things and God's greatest gift, the Holy Spirit, are not flying about somewhere in the world unseen and unheard. They come to us, using the vehicles of definitely earthly mediums, spoken words, printed books (Bible), water (Baptism), bread and wine (Lord's Supper). It became customary to summarise this principle by coining the Latin expression, *Finitum capax infiniti*—secular, earthly, transient things can contain and transfer infinite, eternal things.

---

[1] For references, see Holl, *op. cit.*, pp. 81–4.

[2] cf. H. Sasse, *Was heisst lutherisch*, pp. 94ff., and *Here We Stand*, p. 106; Elert, *op. cit.*, I, 263–80.

The manner in which Luther relates the bread and wine in the Lord's Supper with the body and blood of Christ makes this principle clear. If one could compare the bread with iron and the body of Christ with fire, Luther says: "the Host in the Lord's Supper is like glowing iron," for every part of it means both iron and fire at the same time. "Fire" as such (apart from any substance), does not exist, there is only a burning or glowing substance. In this way, divine gifts are bestowed on us through the vehicles of bread and wine charged with divine power through Christ, who is really present in them during the Lord's Supper.[1] The modern example of a "wire charged with electricity" may still better explain the same truth.

Luther emphatically repudiates the Zwinglian conception that the Lord's Supper has a symbolical meaning only. To return to Luther's example above, this would mean that the iron *symbolises* fire only. It will transfer the divine activities into a sphere beyond our present realities and earthly substances only.

But also the Roman Catholic doctrine of "transubstantiation" cannot easily be reconciled with Luther's principle.[2] It would mean that the iron ceases to exist and fire only remains. Luther is afraid that behind this conception there is an attempt to deny the importance of our present earthly substances. He thinks that there is the same tendency which under-estimates the importance of matrimony and ordinary worldly occupations in favour of the "purely spiritual" ascetic life. But as long as we live on earth we cannot escape material substances like bread and wine. The Spirit works through earthly mediums. Only beyond this earth, in an eschatological world, can we expect a life of merely spiritual bodies freed from material substances. To deny the continued existence of the substance of bread in the Lord's Supper is not only a plain disobedience against the Bible (I Cor. x. 16), but is also an attempt to anticipate the last things too soon. Real bread and the real body of Christ are both present in the Lord's Supper. The term "consubstantiation" has been coined to cover Luther's doctrine. But it is important to know that Luther's repudiation of Zwingli's symbolic conception was much stronger than his fight against "transubstantiation."[3] He thinks that the Pope invents a lot of unnecessary and misleading theories in connection with the Sacraments, whilst Zwingli and others practically abolish the Sacraments altogether.

The same principle also applies to the relations between man and wife in matrimony. Luther rejects the degradation of matrimony to a purely carnal, materialistic affair, but he also

---

[1] *W.A.*, 6,510; *Tischr.*, 96.   [2] *W.A.*, 6,508ff.
[3] See below, p. 123, note 3; cf. McKinnon, *op. cit.*, III, 306–28.

deeply distrusts the so-called affinity of soul between man and wife and the many attempts to represent the sexual relationship in matrimony as something inferior. Luther thinks that the celibacy of the clergy and the over-estimation of the ascetic life of monks and nuns are based on this mistaken conception.[1]

We could trace this principle of Luther's in many instances, and we will later again refer to it in connection with his doctrine of the Holy Scriptures. But the most fateful consequences were the conflicts arising from this principle in the Lord's Supper. Many people cannot understand why Luther so violently rejected Zwingli's brotherhood after both reformers had agreed on almost all the articles of the Christian Creed, seemingly for the sole reason that they could not agree on the doctrine of the Lord's Supper. That Luther allowed Protestant unity to lapse for this reason is often considered to be a proof of his obstinacy and political stupidity. But when Luther was certain that he could not come to terms with Zwingli on this point he did not say, "Zwingli's doctrine on the Lord's Supper is different from mine," but he did say: "Zwingli's spirit is different from mine."[2] He was sure that this one difference revealed a totally different outlook in all spheres of theology, and so were later Lutherans when they mistrusted Calvin's doctrine of the Lord's Supper (which seemed much nearer to Luther than Zwingli's), or when they refused intercommunion with the Church of England on the ground of the "black rubric" in the Book of Common Prayer or for the sake of Article XXVIII, which claims that the Body of Christ is given, taken and eaten only after a heavenly and spiritual manner. They allowed themselves to be accused of causing schisms in Protestantism rather than yield on this point, as they thought that the most vital issues were at stake.

With regard to his disputes with the Roman Catholics, Luther thought that the hair-splitting discussions on "substances" and "accidents" were caused through the influence of pagan philosophy on the Roman Church.[3] He specially accuses Aristotle, "that monster," "that blind heathen" for spoiling Christian theology.[4] I think many scholars will agree that there is something in his suspicions that pagan (especially Neo-Platonist) philosophy influencing Christian theology caused a certain contempt for

[1] cf. Luther's many writings on the celibacy of the clergy, on matrimony, etc., e.g. *W.A.*, 12, 232ff.; *Tischr.*, 433, 3,983, 4,138, 5,282; H. Asmussen, *Seelsorge*, München, 1935, pp. 110–56, esp. pp. 125f.

[2] Luther himself deeply regrets his disagreement with Zwingli, but when Zwingli died he dared not hope that he had gone to Heaven. *Tischr.*, 128f.; cf. also Hildebrandt, *Est, das Lutherische Prinzip.* (*op. cit.*).

[3] *W.A.*, 6,509–11.

[4] *Tischr.*, 155, 5,440; *W.A.*, 6,457f.

material things, for the world of flesh and blood and substance. This may also be the reason why in colloquial Christian speech the conception of "the resurrection of the body" was sometimes replaced by "the immortality of the soul."[1]

8. Sacraments

It is not surprising that Luther lays very strong emphasis on the importance of the sacraments.[2] This is not only caused by his conviction that God deals with us through the medium of earthly things (*finitum capax infiniti*) but also by his belief that we are saved by God's grace alone, not by our own merits and worthiness. Nothing could better illustrate this conception than sacraments which we *receive*. This is especially obvious in the case of infant baptism, the infant being passive. Luther thinks that the true sacrament must be instituted by Christ himself, must contain a promise towards the receiver and an external sign. This sign must be connected with the text to be read or proclaimed during the sacramental action, to make clear the promise of God attached to that sacrament. After some consideration, Luther ultimately arrived at the conclusion that this condition is only fulfilled by baptism and the Lord's Supper. For some time he was inclined to count absolution among the sacraments. But as there was no external sign attached to absolution by Christ, Luther finally no longer counted this as a sacrament. He still attached, however, a high value to absolution, and that is the reason why we treat it under this heading. Some Lutherans, including Melanchthon, inclined to the view that ordination could be called a sacrament. Melanchthon's view was included in the *Apologia* (one of the official Lutheran Confessions), but this was not generally accepted, as ordination does not appear to fulfil Luther's conditions for a sacrament any more than absolution.

This high estimation of sacraments was not universal in later Lutheranism. While some branches of the Lutheran Church kept the sacraments in high esteem, other branches, at certain times (especially in the periods of Pietism and Enlightenment) were inclined to think that Luther's high estimation of the sacraments was a mediæval survival and could not be reconciled with the rest of his reforms. While Luther thinks that a Christian who does not make his Communion at least four times a year very likely by his

[1] *Tischr.*, 5,230.

[2] The following description of Luther's doctrine on the sacraments is in the main based on his book, *De captivitate Babylonica Ecclesiae praeludium*, 1520; *W.A.*, 6, 497–573. Cf. Köstlin, *op. cit.*, II, 230–56; Elert, *op. cit.*, I, 255–80.

abstaining indicates his lack of Christian faith,[1] later Lutherans often only attended this sacrament a few times during the whole of their life. At the present time we have a clear reaction against this under-estimation. Modern Lutheran writings and Church practice alike show a revival of Luther's original sacramental ideas. What in former times were considered to be "mediæval survivals" in Luther, are now often considered to be essential parts of his doctrine. This applies not only to the sacraments, but to other precepts as well.

To give a fairly comprehensive description of Luther's doctrine of the sacraments would require a book of its own. We can only indicate a few characteristic ideas.

9. *Baptism*

Luther thinks that many Christians have been misled by the saying of St. Jerome, "that penitence was the second plank after shipwreck." This would imply that if the ship of baptism was wrecked through sin, penitence, or other means of grace, had to take its place in order to save the sinner from being drowned. The whole mediæval system of good works, vows, pilgrimages and an ascetic life, he thinks, were attempts to save by other means people whose baptism had become wrecked and meaningless. But his belief is that baptism can never be wrecked. It stands on *God's* promise, and our own unworthiness cannot destroy that promise. Even children may receive this promise.[2] The ship of our baptism (or the ship of the Church whose members we become through baptism) can never sink. It must arrive at the port of Heaven. Through sin we abandon the ship and jump into the sea, where we are in danger of being drowned. The true meaning of penitence must be to draw us back into the ship, and recover the blessings of baptism. Baptism is the basic sacrament, and we need, during the whole of our life, to return to it again and again, if we are to fulfil the benefits bestowed on us by it.

The pouring of water in baptism has the same meaning as full immersion in New Testament times, viz. that a man is drowned in baptism and a new man emerges. Luther does not think that the ritual of full immersion is necessary; our present practice means the same. From the day of our baptism, we have to die from all ungodliness during the whole of our lives, and daily we have to be re-born. Baptism "signifies that the old Adam in us should, by daily contrition and repentance, be drowned and die with all

---

[1] Preface to Shorter Catechism.
[2] Elert, *op. cit.*, II, 259f.; cf. *Tischr.*, 549, 3,608.

sins and evil lusts, and, again, a new man daily come forth and arise, who shall live before God in righteousness and purity for ever."

10. *Absolution*[1]

But do the sacraments not demand faith on our part? Does God through His grace save us automatically through sacramental ritual *ex opere operato*? No. Luther very clearly demands faith on our part. And yet the validity of the sacraments does not depend on our faith, but on God's promise.

This is especially clearly shown in Luther's teaching on absolution, and it is for this reason that I here add some lines on absolution, in spite of the fact that absolution is not a sacrament.

For Luther absolution is always closely connected with confession, but while he thinks that absolution is instituted by Christ, confession and its various uses were instituted as a good healthy order of the Church. Luther thinks that private confession is a very good institution and wishes it preserved with two alterations from the mediæval practice: (1) It is impossible to confess *all* sins.[2] Our whole attitude, our feelings and thoughts are sinful, but enumeration of the sins we remember and recognise would only reveal part of our sinful life. Therefore the necessity to confess every sin led either to an oppression of conscience or to self-delusion. The Church should only expect us to confess those sins which are on our minds. (2) Confession ought not to be compulsory, but voluntary. Luther thinks that a minister ought to examine a communicant before admitting him for the first time to the Lord's Table, but this is not a case of ordinary confession only, but a combination of confession and the above-mentioned examination (which ultimately led to the revival of confirmation). On the whole, Luther himself made his confession before receiving the Lord's Supper,[3] but consciously he made occasional exceptions to this rule as he did not want to make an order requiring confession before the Lord's Supper. The confessional was not regarded as being based on a divine institution.[4]

For several decades private confession was generally preserved in Lutheranism, but later on in many parts (practically the whole of Germany) it fell victim to Pietism, Rationalism and

---

[1] Luther's attitude to confession and absolution is well described in G. Rietschel, *Lehrbuch der Liturgik*, Vol. II, Berlin, 1909, pp. 366–85; see also under "The Office of the Keys" in Luther's Catechisms.

[2] e.g. *Tischr.*, 5,175; cf. Augsbg. Conf., Art. XI.

[3] This was a general Lutheran practice; see Augsb. Conf., Art. XXV.

[4] Luther rigidly maintains the duty of the minister to preserve the secrecy of confession, even if questioned by State authorities, e.g. *Tischr.*, 5,178. This led to a recent conflict between the Church of Norway and the Quisling Government.

Calvinism. There are now many attempts to revive private confession.

Since the Reformation there have been attempts to introduce "general confession" and "public absolution" of the whole congregation in Church as an alternative to private confession.[1] Luther himself occasionally used this form, but was apparently not quite happy about it. Under his very eyes, it was abolished in Wittenberg, but later on became practically the universal form of confession and absolution in Lutheranism.

Luther thinks that *private* absolution is valid unconditionally. It rests on the ground of God's promise and not on the honesty of the confessing sinner. It is, he says, like a castle that has been presented to me in a legal way. I am the legal owner of that castle, whether I use it or not, whether I am worthy and make good use of it or not. But it will only bring me advantages if I make good use of it.

It is the same with regard to God's Absolution. A man is the legal owner of the absolution proclaimed to him through the minister of the Church, but it depends on his faith whether he believes in this gift and makes good use of it.

But this applies only to private confession and absolution. It is not quite the same as in the General Confession which the congregation recite together in Church. This gives no opportunity to the minister to explore the mind of the individual. For this reason, the absolution proclaimed by Luther after the General Confession is conditioned: "I as a Vicar absolve all those here present who are listening to the Word of God and believe in our Lord Jesus Christ and are truly penitent."[2]

11. *The Lord's Supper*

Luther starts from the word, "This is the New Testament in my Blood." A testament pre-supposes three things: (1) a testator knows he has to die; (2) he enumerates his possessions; (3) he authorises the receivers of his heritage.

God makes a testament which shows that God wants to die. But God cannot die; only man can die. So that the expression "the New Testament in my Blood," briefly indicates that God, having become man, wishes to die for the benefit of others. The heritage

---

[1] The whole congregation speaks together a confession of sins, for which there is a fixed formula; alternatively the minister speaks it for the congregation and then asks the congregation whether they identify themselves with this confession and desire the forgiveness of sin. The whole congregation answers, "Yes," whereupon the minister pronounces the general absolution.

[2] cf. G. Rietschel, *ibid.*, pp. 382-4.

He left at His death is "Forgiveness of sins, life and salvation ... for where there is forgiveness of sins there is also life and salvation." This heritage is the possession of those who receive the sacrament and believe God's promise attached to it. It is as if a rich man leaves a large sum to a poor beggar. The sum belongs to the beggar, not by virtue of his dignity, but by virtue of the rich man's testament; but the beggar, believing in this testament, accepts the sum.

Luther's emphasis on the sacraments cannot easily be accepted by those Reformed theologians who over-emphasise the doctrine of pre-destination. If it is clear from the very beginning by decree of God that while one man is saved another is lost, the sacraments lose their value as real means of grace, being no longer able to bring about an effective change in man. If it is certain that I am lost, the sacrament does not help me nor can it bring additional loss to me—it is just nothing. If it is decided that I shall be saved, the sacrament might strengthen me, but it can cause no change of real importance.

Therefore Luther in his later years, and many Lutherans, disliked speculation in too great detail about pre-destination. He preferred to encourage and to invite people "to believe that the sacrament can and will save them." He thinks that not only the believer, but even the unbeliever, receives the true Sacrament effectively. If man is seriously longing for Christ, the sacrament will help him. If he comes as a hypocrite and without serious intention, it will hurt him. But it is never without meaning and effect.

12. *Law and Gospel*[1]

As we have seen, Luther thinks that the preaching of the Gospel will create faith. But, one may ask, can people understand the saving Gospel before having understood that they are sinners? And can they understand that they are sinners before they understand the seriousness of God's Law, against which they have sinned? Luther therefore defends the duty of the true Church to preach the Law as well as the Gospel in face of the opposition put up by Agricola and other friends of his.

There are apparently two main lines of thought in the Bible: (i) God has given man a Law and he must fulfil it or be condemned. (ii) On the other hand, man cannot fulfil the Law of God and can only be saved by grace alone (Gospel). One has to take both lines seriously; but the main question of theology is how to relate them to each other.

[1] Köstlin, *op. cit.*, II, 224ff.; *Popular Symbolics* (*op. cit.*), pp. 78–82.

Traditionally, Lutheran theologians speak of three uses of the Law: *Primus, secundus et tertius usus legis*. Luther himself usually mentioned two uses of the Law, but he refers to all three. *Primus usus legis* means that the Law must be used as a foundation for the standards of life, of general morals in public and private affairs. We must never forget that Luther very often preached and wrote about the Ten Commandments and tried to influence the morals of his time, including even economic and political ethics. To use the Law in this way means *coercere impios*. He also calls the first use of the Law *usus civilis legis*. This raises the problem whether for Luther there was such a thing as a Christian "civilisation." While Anglo-Saxon theologians like to speak about Christian civilisation, quite a number of Continental theologians have an extreme aversion to this expression. Even if this term could be interpreted as referring to the first use of the Law, the question may be asked, how far this use is typically "Christian." Do not even decent Jews and pagans use the Law in the same way?

Secundus usus legis. Christ has shown us that it is not enough to use the Law in an external, literal sense only. He made it clear that wrath has the same meaning as murder, and evil lust the same meaning as adultery in the eyes of God. If we take the Laws of God as seriously as the Sermon on the Mount requires, if we really try to love our neighbour (even the hated Samaritan and publican) as ourselves, we soon will realise how sinful we are. And it is not enough "to do one's best." The Law threatens every one with condemnation who does not *completely* fulfil all parts of it. If we take the Law seriously according to Christ's interpretation, we have to admit that none of us ever can fulfil it. This is expressed in one of the first Lutheran hymns by Paul Speratus: "It was a wrong conception that God has given His law as if we could fulfil it by our own efforts. Rather is it only a mirror, showing us our sinful character."[1] If we realise all this, the Law will drive us into anxiety and despair. We shall feel as if we had been thrown into hell. We will be terrified by God's wrath.[2] This anxiety and despair presumably will cause us to seek for salvation. It will lead us to the Gospel. For Luther, salvation always comes out of hell.[3] In the terrified soul, the Gospel will create faith. This process of conversion is described by Luther in these terms:

[1] Hymn, "*Es ist das Heil uns kommen her*" (*Dtsch. Ev. Gesangbuch*, No. 149, verse 3).

[2] Elert, *op. cit.*, I, 31ff. "*Die Angst mich zu verzweifeln trieb/ dass nichts denn sterben bei mir blieb/ zur Hoelle musst' ich sinken*" (*Dtsch. Ev. Gesangbuch*, No. 148, verse 3).

[3] *Ibid.*, verse 4 (*Da jammert Gott in Ewigkeit/ mein Elend uebermassen*, etc.). Cf. Elert, *ibid.*, 39ff.

"I believe that I cannot by my own reason or strength believe in Jesus Christ, my Lord, or come to Him; but the Holy Ghost has called me by the Gospel, enlightened me with His gifts, sanctified and kept me in true faith; even as He calls, gathers, enlightens and sanctifies the whole Christian Church on earth and keeps it with Jesus Christ in the one true faith: in which Christian Church He daily and richly forgives all sins to me and all believers. . . ."[1]

Tertius usus legis. While the Law is indispensable for creating faith, the question will arise whether it is still of any value to the believer. We have seen that the believer's faith implies his unity with Christ (he becomes one cake with Christ), and that the Holy Spirit provides him with guidance and illumination. Does this mean that the believer has no need of the Law any longer; that he is directly led by Christ and the Holy Spirit? Some of Luther's contemporaries thought that he had not clearly answered that question. But I think it is clearly implied in his writings and teaching that the Law has still some value for the believer, but not in a narrow legalistic sense. I would say: it is like a compass, indicating the general direction of a journey, not like a detailed map prescribing certain roads. It teaches the believer to control himself. In this sense, the latest confessional writing, the *Formula Concordiae*, attaches doctrine to the Law in its third use.

Some theologians think that in Luther's opinion the Christian is completely free from the Law, even from a kind of third use of the Law as described in the preceding lines. But no man is ever a *complete* Christian *only*: we are, on the one hand, saved Christians and at the same time again and again sinners. This latter fact accounts for our need to resort continuously to the second use of the Law, whilst, on the other hand, as Christians we are free from the Law. This point is stressed in contemporary Scandinavian theology.

"The *Formula of Concord* is as consistent as Luther in its teaching that the Christian is free from all that is called Law.

"That Law still has its place in the life of the Christian—and that is what the *Formula of Concord* tries to express by its doctrine of the third use of the Law—is motivated by the fact that the Christian is not only a new man, but also at the same time the old man, not only saved, but also at the same time sinner, not only spirit but also flesh."[2]

[1] Shorter Catechism, On Second Article.
[2] R. Bring, quoted from a book review in *Svensk Kyrkotidning*, 39th Year, No. 20, Uppsala, May 20th, 1943.

We must never underestimate the importance attached by Luther to the need for seeing Law and Gospel in their right relation. The whole theology of Luther, including his doctrine of justification and his attitude to the Bible, can only be understood by those who have grasped the meaning of the distinction and relation between Law and Gospel. For this reason, I should like to deal more fully with this subject, but the space of this book does not permit me to do so. There is, however, a good opportunity for English-speaking Christians to gain a better insight into this problem if they will refer to a recent short publication which is devoted exclusively to this subject.[1]

13. *The letter and the spirit*[2]

Although Luther has a high regard for the importance of the Law, he does not insist on a too-legalistic, narrow interpretation. It is not sufficient to fulfil the letter of the Law but it is necessary and often much more difficult to fulfil the spirit behind the Law.[3]

Christ states that no one should "put away his wife save for the cause of fornication." Luther clearly accepts this command as binding. For the Christian, divorce ought not to take place except for fornication. But Luther makes it clear that in certain cases divorce might be the lesser evil in the eyes of God although the cause was not actually adultery. On the other hand, there may be cases of a wife betraying her husband when divorce would not be justified, and where forgiveness would set things right.

Thus Luther, during the course of his life, sanctioned many cases of divorce. If a wife left her husband without substantial reason, Luther, as a representative of the Church, would send her an ultimatum demanding her return by a certain date, and if she did not comply with this, he would declare the husband free to divorce her, and able to marry again. He justified this by quoting Biblical passages which showed that God had instituted matrimony for the protection of man against evil lust, and that it was a breach of God's command to force a man to live unmarried for ever because his wife would not return to him.[4]

---

[1] A. R. Vidler, *Christ's Strange Work*, the Bishop of London's Lent Book, 1944.

[2] On the whole question of ethics in Luther's theology, see Holl, *op. cit.*, pp. 155–287 (*Der Neubau der Sittlichkeit*).

[3] *Kirchenpostille*, On Second Corinthians iii. 4–11; 12. *post Trin.*; cf. Speratus; "*Vom Fleisch wollt' nicht heraus der Geist/ vom Gesetz erfordert allermeist/ es war mit uns verloren*" (*Dtsch. Ev. Gesangbuch*, No. 149, verse 2).

[4] Cf. *W.A.*, 6, 550–60; divorce is allowed in case of incurable disease of one partner, *Briefw.*, No. 1,134, August 23rd, 1527; cf. *Popular Symbolics*, *op. cit.*, pp. 123f.

THE DOCTRINE OF SALVATION

Another example of Luther's principles in such matters is afforded by the following: If, after marriage, the wife discovers that her husband is impotent (and had previously concealed this fact from her), the wife is either allowed divorce or is not condemned if she takes a man in place of her husband.[1]

Many Christians in Europe were shocked by these ideas,[2] and most later Lutherans did not accept them, but apologised for Luther, explaining that he may have evolved these ideas in reaction against the discouragement and prevention of marriage imposed by the complicated system of Roman Church law. This explanation certainly is partly true, and in the later years of his life Luther seems to have been more conservative on this point. And yet he never changed completely. He does not claim that God's Laws could ever be set aside, but rather that in these complicated cases there were conflicts between the various rules given in the Word of God.[3] Sin could not be avoided by rigidly applying the *letter* of *one* Law, but rather by taking into account the *spirit* behind *all* Laws.[4] In facing the facts, he is a realist, and this realism opens his eyes to the vast complications created by sin in the world,[5] and he affirmed that sinfulness cannot be cured by the Law, but only by the Gospel.

The principle that it is not the letter but the spirit of the Law that matters should render Luther's Church very well able to adapt herself to most of the various forms of political, social and economic life. On the other hand, it renders the Lutheran Church somewhat defenceless against powerful law-breakers who give a fairly plausible explanation of their law-breaking.

In all countries in Europe which were put under National-Socialist régimes, so-called sterilisation laws were introduced to prevent people with hereditary disease from having children. Many people suspected that the misuse of these laws might be enormous and that they would be used merely as a pretext for

---

[1] *W.A.*, 6, 558.

[2] "His utterances on sexual morality escape censure by being absolutely unprintable," W. R. Inge, "German Protestantism," in the *Church of England Newspaper*, August 4th, 1944.

[3] Cf. e.g. Luther's disputed attitude in the case of the bigamy of the Elector Philip of Hessen. *Tischr.*, 5,038; "*Digamia hoc habet exemplum in scriptura...*," *Tischr.*, 5,046, but Luther feels that this precedence is highly dangerous, *Tischr.*, 5,088b, 5,096; *Briefw.*, No. 1,056, November 28th, 1526; *W.A.*, 53, 190ff. "*Es ist ein hohes Wagnis*," *Tischr.*, 5,046; cf. McKinnon, *op cit.*, IV, 265-72.

[4] e.g. children ought to ask the parents' consent before getting married. But if the parents withhold their consent unreasonably the children can disobey them. *W.A.*, 15, 163ff., *Briefw.*, April 4th, 1539; Luther marries a couple against the (unreasonable) decision of the bride's father, *Tischr.*, 5,441.

[5] Luther has on various occasions refused to condemn people who had committed suicide in desperate circumstances, *Tischr.*, 150, 222, 5,546.

destroying the posterity of political opponents and for the extermination of hated races.

The Roman Catholic Church condemned any kind of interference with the body of man by sterilisation or similar means as un-Christian. She knew no compromise; in her view, even people of total mental deficiency whose habit it was to do violence to women should not be sterilised.

Lutherans had to admit that there might be cases in which operations of this kind might be the lesser evil, but, having once admitted this, the Lutherans were weakened in their power of total resistance. This shows that the Lutheran emphasis on the spirit rather than on the letter of the Law may in certain circumstances weaken the opposition to misuse. It is, however, fair to note that the Roman Church also had to compromise in the end: after having protested in vain, the Roman Church did not carry the matter to its logical conclusion, i.e. by breaking off relations with all those responsible for these laws.

A proverb of rather doubtful value summarises Luther's attitude towards the Law of God and the good works of man in this way, *Lustig gelebt und selig gestorben* (Live in pleasure and die a saved man). But Luther not only avoided saying anything of this sort; his conception of Living Faith makes it impossible for man to claim to be a believer and yet not to recognise God's Law and to try with all his power to keep it. As a good tree is bound to bring forth good fruit, so a good faith is bound to produce good works as the fruit of faith. But a good tree does not become a fruit tree by bringing forth its fruit; it was a fruit tree before, and from its bearing of fruit we recognise this fact. A believing Christian does not become a Christian by doing good works: he was already a Christian, and we recognise this fact by his life.[1]

As we have seen, it is obvious that Luther, when judging people's behaviour, makes much allowance for contradictory duties. It is wrong to kill people, but it is the lesser evil to defend Europe by force of arms against the Mohammedan aggression of the Turks, who in his time threatened to destroy the Christian peoples of Europe. It is interesting that Karl Barth, when inviting the Christian Churches to preach the war against Fascism, expressly justifies his attitude by referring to Luther's activities against the Turks.[2] There are other cases where Luther advises Christians to choose the lesser evil. Confronted with a choice between two courses, which both involve a certain amount of sin, the Christian should take the line which seems to involve the least amount of sinning and to console his conscience by remembering that for

[1] *Bekenntnisschriften*, pp. 311f.; cf. A. R. Vidler, *op. cit.*, pp. 53f.
[2] K. Barth, *Die Kirche und die politische Frage von heute*, Zollikon, 1939, 41f., 50.

these unavoidable sins there is forgiveness by God through the Cross.

A typical example of this principle is his attitude to war and conscientious objection:[1]

1. War is an evil, a consequence of human sin.[2]

2. In certain circumstances, it may be the lesser evil. In an operation, it may be necessary to cut off a man's arm in order to save his body; God asks us to help our neighbour. Christian charity may demand such an operation. In the same way, war may be a necessary operation in order to save the life of a state and of innocent citizens.

3. But it is the lesser evil only if it is a "just" war of defence, not a war of aggression or lust for power. The war must be ordered by the lawful government to whom God has entrusted the sword, and not by private enterprise.

4. If a Christian is convinced that the war is "unjust," he must refuse military service. The decision, whether a war is just or unjust, therefore, lies ultimately in the conscience of the individual.

5. This means, of course, that the individual has to bear the consequences. It would be better for him to suffer persecution and even death at the hands of his own government as the result of his conscientious objection, than to take part in a war which to his conscience is unjust. For it is better to lose his body and his possessions than to disobey his conscience.

6. If, however, a Christian is in doubt as to the justice of the war, he should leave the responsibility to his own government. In this case the government is responsible before God. (This last point very often serves as an excuse for blind obedience in every war. But Luther thought that this danger could be avoided.)

Luther's expression, *"pecca fortiter"*[3] (sin courageously) is often quoted as an argument against him, but it does not mean that Luther thought people should "sin courageously" in order to enable God to show His mercy and grace by much forgiveness of sins. Only great ignorance can suggest anything of that sort. Why

---

[1] *W.A.*, 11, 245–80; 19, 623–62; cf. 6,265.

[2] War machines are an invention of the devil. *Tischr.*, 3,552.

[3] For quotations and argument, see Holl, *op. cit.*, 235ff.

should he always have emphasised the Ten Commandments and the need for a moral life? Luther sees clearly that in a terrible world even *good* acts involve sin. One cannot defend the Christian people of Europe against the Turks without violence and slaughter. A good prince, who wants to protect his good subjects, might be faced with the necessity of using force and showing hardness and severity. In similar conflicts, whenever we have done all we can to find the lesser evil and discover God's will, we should not despair, even if we know that on earth we cannot avoid sinning. We should face this fact in a realistic way, *pecca fortiter*, and console our hearts with the knowledge that there is forgiveness of sins.

14. *Distinction between Law and Gospel*

Now we should understand why Luther makes a definite distinction between the Law and the Gospel. He resists those who think that they can be saved by fulfilling laws and by doing good works. Even in his hymns he stresses the point that the Law cannot be fulfilled by any human being, but only by Christ who fulfilled it for us. But Luther also attacks his friend Agricola, and others who wished to abolish the Law and replace it by the Gospel. Both are vital. Only men terrified by the Law can grasp the Gospel; only a man saved by the Gospel is released from the tyranny of the Law. There must be no confusion between the Law and the Gospel.

Rightly or wrongly, therefore, Luther's followers were and are afraid that Catholics and Calvinists show a tendency to use the Gospel as a law book, and make the New Testament a foundation, not only for the constitution of the Church, but also of the State. But the fruits of the Holy Spirit which may be looked for in a changed and converted believer cannot be turned into laws, and made to serve as the basis for the social life of people who in practice are not believers. The principles of the Gospel cannot be transformed into *Laws*, to provide statutes for a new international world order, or the constitution of a new League of Nations. This may be one reason why many contemporary Lutherans are disquieted by the way some Christians discuss world reconstruction after the war. Can there be any relation between Christian love (charity as described in 1 Cor. xiii.), and tribunals for trying war criminals? Or between 1 Cor. xiii and State or world constitutions, in a situation where real Christians are only a small minority?

Law and justice have their proper place, and so has the Gospel; but the Gospel cannot be made a Law for the general public.

Judges and tribunals cannot be governed by the Gospel principle of "forgiveness of sins"; they are in the sphere of the Law. Nor can the Law be made a Gospel; man cannot be saved by keeping laws; there is no "justification by decency." Confusion between the Law and the Gospel makes Christians lose that sober sense of reality which is indispensable in this world.

IV

THE CHURCH AS THE BODY OF CHRIST—THE MINISTRY

1. *What is the Church?*[1]

LUTHER and his followers were accused of splitting the Church by their breaking away from the papal authority, the Roman Catholic episcopacy and liturgy. Luther would answer by stressing two aspects:

(a) *A negative aspect:* The unity of the Church is not *created* by uniformity of constitution or ceremonies, and it is not *broken* by variety of constitution or ceremonies.

(b) *A positive aspect:* The Church is the body of Christ. Members of the body are all true believers wherever they may be found. If the true believers are found in different denominations, they are yet *one* in faith belonging to the *one* body of Christ in spite of denominational divisions. If, however, true believers and unbelievers are found side by side in one and the same denomination, they yet are not members of the same Church—not one in faith.

The Church is the Body of Christ. What does it mean? (a) By stressing the word *Christ*, it means: Christ, the Head of the Body, moves and rules His members by the Spirit. (b) By stressing the word *"body"*, it means: the Church is the Body formed of those who believe, who have faith. They form the so-called Communion of Saints. These two things mean the same: being moved by Christ, and having faith.

2. *Visible and invisible Church*[1]

The Church is invisible in so far as it is impossible to look into men's hearts. The Church consists of all those human beings who have faith.

There is, however, only one way to create faith, to create believing men: by the instruments of Word and Sacraments. But faith is no secure and lifeless possession like a jewel; it is a living thing based on daily repentance and daily regeneration. God daily creates faith in a man's heart, as the sun daily creates the light of

---

[1] On the whole subject, cf. Elert, *op. cit.*, I, 224–335; Köstlin, *op. cit.*, II, 256–90, 304f.; Holl, *op. cit.*, 288–325; Th. Harnack, *Die Kirche, ihr Amt, ihr Regiment*, Nürnberg, 1862; McKinnon, *op. cit.*, III, 280ff.

the moon. For this reason, God must continually create faith even in a believing man's heart, i.e. even the believing man needs the presence of Christ in Word and Sacrament.

Word and Sacrament are therefore essential: (a) in order to create faith, and (b) in order to maintain faith in the believer.

Thus the Church Invisible is a fellowship of all those many believers in all countries and denominations whom God alone knows. It is *created* and *maintained* by Word and Sacrament. For as the Augsburg Confession says: "By Word and Sacraments as by instruments, the Holy Spirit creates faith *where and when it pleases God.*"[1]

This *"ubi et quando visum est Deo"* means that we cannot use Word and Sacrament, or any kind of episcopal laying-on of hands, as the means by which we can *force* the Holy Spirit to create faith in a person. It has pleased God in His freedom to bind Himself to Word and Sacrament as to the instruments by which the Holy Spirit creates faith: but in each case it must be left to Him whether, where, when and how, He will make use of this Word proclaimed by us and the Sacrament administered by us to create faith.

The fact that the Church is created and maintained, that believers are in existence, is therefore indicated to the outside world by the fact that people listen to a sermon, that somebody is preaching, that people are celebrating the Lord's Supper, and baptising infants or adults.

Thus the Church Invisible has *externae notae* (external marks) that are distinctly visible and audible. For Word and Sacrament are living things: they are action. "Word" does not mean a Bible lying about in the library; it means the Word preached, *viva vox evangelii*, the living voice of the Gospel.[2] "Sacrament" means the Sacrament administered.

The study of Luther's liturgical writings clearly shows the strong connection between the proclaimed Word (preaching) and the sacramental act. The Sacrament is *verbum visibile*; it has to make visible, to confirm the preached Word, to put God's seal under God's promise. The mere reading of a lesson without proper preaching is not sufficient. Here we should understand the mistrust felt by Lutherans (and other Protestants) of Churches in which the Sacrament is frequently celebrated without a sermon. The Word that ought to be made visible and confirmed by God's seal has not been properly proclaimed. It became Lutheran practice to insist on proper preaching in connection, not only

[1] Augsbg. Conf., Art. V.
[2] e.g. *W.A.*, 21, 466, 36; *Tischr.*, 4,081. (*Mirabilis profecto potentia verbi vocalis*) *Tischr.*, 4,121.

with the Sacraments, but with all Church acts, e.g. marriages, funerals, etc.

The true Church is always Visible and Invisible alike. My example would be, the hidden, invisible and inaudible electricity in a cloud is again and again bound to become visible in lightning and thunder; for there is no lightning without thunder, no lightning and thunder without electricity. Similarly the Invisible Church, composed of people who have their faith unseen in their hearts, is bound to become visible and audible again and again in its functions, Word and Sacrament. It is, therefore, misleading to say that the true Church is Invisible only. It is both Invisible and Visible.

3. *True Apostolic succession*

But not *any* kind of preaching or sacramental practice will do. Only the pure and true doctrine, the pure and right administration of the sacraments, will be likely to create true faith and a truly believing Church. And *vice versa* only a truly believing Church can produce the pure and right administration of Word and Sacrament. What causes the splitting of the Church Visible into denominations is mainly difference of opinion concerning the question: how true faith can be created. It is the question: what is the true and pure Word; which is the right administration of the sacraments?

Luther admits that even in Churches with doubtful doctrine (like the mediæval Church) the traces of the pure Gospel may still be strong enough to create some real believers. But the wrong doctrine and practice mixed up with the pure doctrine in these Churches will make it difficult for the Holy Spirit to use the Word and Sacrament of such Churches for the creation of faith. Therefore it is the duty of the true Church to do all in her power to provide pure preaching and the pure administration of the sacraments, based on the pure doctrine.[1]

The pure and true doctrine is essentially the same as that of the Apostles who received it from Christ Himself; and the Apostles administered the Sacraments as demanded by Christ Himself. And the true faith created by Word and Sacrament is the same as that held by the Apostles. The existence of the real Church, therefore, is bound to a kind of *Apostolic Succession*.[2]

---

[1] A recent expression of American Lutheran opinion: "The Lutheran Church, the Church of the pure doctrine, makes much of the pure doctrine. She holds it sacred. . . . In matters on which Scripture is silent . . . she readily yields, but she is unyielding where the pure doctrine is concerned. 'The doctrine is not ours, but God's (Luther) and of that which is God's not one jot or tittle can be yielded." *Popular Symbolics* (*op. cit.*), pp. 11f.

[2] *W.A.*, 34, I, 318, 15; 320, 5; "Holy Father, keep them in my name . . ." (John xvii. 11) means: "Dear Father, may it please Thee to protect them from wrong doctrine," *W.A.*, 28, 144ff.

There are three ways in which the term Apostolic Succession is used:

(a) *Succession of properly appointed bishops in a see or diocese.* An Anglican bishop says about St. Augustine: "Succession in fact, with him, meant, as always in the ancient Church, the succession of bishops in a see, and not succession by ordination."[1] This conception would probably include the opinion that new dioceses could only be founded as branches or daughters of already existing mother dioceses. The question whether episcopacy in the sense of the Early Church was something like the present episcopacy, or whether the "bishop" was no more than a local "vicar," was a subject of dispute between Luther and his opponents.

(b) *Succession by Ordination or Consecration.*

(c) *Succession in the* WORK *done by the Apostles and in the* DOCTRINE *of the Apostles.*[2]

It is the third interpretation that is specially stressed by Luther. He does not speak of *Succession* frequently, but when he does, he says: it is the same as "the Gospel."[3]

He also knows the first use of the term, but he does not accept it. On the other hand, I think, he is slightly influenced by it. He does not try to form a free Church with his own vicars and bishops by the side of an existing Church organisation, but he tries to make the existing vicars and bishops Lutheran; failing that, he tries to force their resignation and appoint his own followers in their place. If this method does not succeed, he desists for the time being and advises his followers to leave that district and to take up residence in places where the official vicar preaches the right doctrine. In Augsburg, for instance, the magistrates and all the vicars were followers of the Pope. The Lutherans in that city asked Luther whether they ought to arrange for Lutheran Communion services in a private house. He replied that he did not wholly agree with this idea. If they made this arrangement they should inform the magistrates officially. But Luther would prefer them to attend Communion services at the near-by village where the official vicar was a Lutheran.[4]

---

[1] A. C. Headlam, *The Doctrine of the Church and Reunion* (Bampton Lecture, 1920), p. 160.
[2] On the whole subject, cf. Headlam, *op., cit.* pp. 124ff.
[3] *Evangelium soll die successio sein*, W.A., 39, II, 177, 2; cf. W.A., 6,293, 1; 39, II, 176ff.
[4] *Briefw.*, June 20th, 1533; July 21st, 1533; cf. W.A., 31, I, 211, 11; 41, 546, 11.

We must not overlook the probability that Luther took this line, not only for ecclesiastical reasons, but out of his great fear of riots and tumults which, in his opinion, might easily arise if there were rivalry between Lutherans and Catholics in the same place.

Things are different for a Christian who happens to be stranded in pagan surroundings. He may quite simply start preaching and acting as a missionary and, if he has converted and baptised a number of people, they may elect him to act as their minister.[1]

4. *Church divisions and Church unity*

If the bishop remained Roman Catholic when the clergy and laity became predominantly Lutheran, Luther organised the Church in the diocese on non-episcopal lines, and he had not the slightest scruples in doing so, for he thought it was quite unimportant whether or not there should be *one* liturgical practice and *one* Church order throughout the world, as his opponents demanded. He could put up with most varying forms of Church constitution, ordination and ritual, for these things, he thought, have no relevance whatever to the unity or purity of the Church. This principle of Luther is laid down in Article VII of the Augsburg Confession, and thus is still an official Lutheran doctrine throughout the world. It runs:

> We also teach that there always must be one Holy Christian Church. And the Church is the Communion of Saints in which the Gospel is preached purely and the Sacraments administered rightly. And it is sufficient for the true unity of the Church to have agreement on the doctrine of the Gospel and the administration of the Sacraments. And for the true unity of the Christian Church it is not necessary that the human traditions or rituals or ceremonies are the same everywhere. . . .

If, therefore, Luther was accused of causing divisions in the Church of his day, he would answer that the unity of the Church had been broken long ago because it had allowed doctrines to be proclaimed that contradicted and excluded one another. The unity of the Church was completely broken before Luther, and this fact had been hidden through the apparent uniformity of ceremonies and constitutions.

This point is very vital if we are to understand the deeply-rooted distrust felt by Lutherans towards proposals of Church

[1] *W.A.*, 11, 412, 16; 16, 35.

reunion or of intercommunion on the lines of agreement on episcopacy or ritual. As we have seen (pp. 45f), Lutherans in former times refused inter-communion with the Church of England because they could not ignore what they thought to be "Calvinistic" formulations in the Prayer Book and Articles. Before discussing the question of intercommunion, they demanded a clear unity of doctrine, made evident by the alteration of the Prayer Book and the Articles. Many modern Lutherans will be more tolerant on this point, especially those in Sweden and Prussia, while others, e.g. those in Hanover and Southern Germany and large Lutheran bodies in the United States and Canada, would probably still refuse intercommunion with a Church which does not abolish what they consider "wrong doctrine" in the Prayer Book. For it is the unity of doctrine that matters, not the unity of organisation.

This does not mean that Lutherans would tolerate *every* form of Church constitution or ceremony. Some constitutions (blind obedience to Bishops or Pope, dictatorship in Church affairs) and some ceremonies, are bound to harm the doctrine and work of the Church. But, on the other hand, Luther and his followers know quite a number of workable Church constitutions and rituals which are used up to this day. There are Lutheran Churches with episcopal, presbyterian or congregational constitutions, and some combine these different principles. The question, which particular form of Church government or of ceremonies should be used in this or that province, or in this or that congregation, is not without importance. But the details can be decided by careful and responsible *human* deliberation, bearing in mind the actual situation in which the Church finds itself in the different countries and at various times. The question whether *unity* of ritual is desirable or not, ought to be decided in the same way. Some Lutheran Churches adopted a uniformity of ritual for a whole country (Sweden). In Germany, however, the various provinces (*Landeskirchen*) use different Prayer Books (Hanover, Saxony, etc.), and some give freedom to every congregation to adopt its own liturgy (Hamburg). Though variety may have many disadvantages,[1] Luther thinks there is *one* advantage: the variety shows where the unity of the Church does *not* lie.[2] Luther was even afraid of having his Wittenberg Liturgy printed.[3] He feared that his followers would copy it and a new wrong uniformity might arise in that the unalterable Roman Mass was replaced by the

[1] *Briefw.*, March 21st, 1534.
[2] *W.A.*, 19, 72ff.; Luther wears different vestments in his two churches, *W.A.*, 18, 113, 5; cf. Holl, *op. cit.*, 361ff.; Elert, *op. cit.*, I, 290f.
[3] *W.A.*, 19, 44ff.; 26, 175.

unalterable Liturgy of Wittenberg;[1] and he violently opposed the idea of creating uniformity by calling together a Lutheran Church Assembly which should make laws on ceremonial questions.[2]

5. *Valid ministries and broken "Apostolic Succession"*

True Apostolic Succession means: people are made Christians, and to some extent successors of the Apostles, by sharing the Apostles' faith. This faith is created by pure Word and Sacraments as entrusted to the Church by the Apostles of Christ. And this faith constantly requires and brings forth continuous preaching of the Word and administration of the Sacraments. And all this is based on the great acts of God in Christ, on the "Gospel," the *Evangelium*; this is truly "evangelical."

Where this state of affairs exists, there the true Apostolic Succession exists, there the Church as the Body of Christ exists— with or without episcopal consecration. And where this state of affairs does *not* exist, there the Apostolic Succession is broken, and the ministering of the Church is invalidated in spite of all bishops and their consecrations.[3]

Let us take a brief selection of Luther's sayings concerning this point: "The reason for believing in a bishop is not the fact that he is the successor of the bishop of that place, but the fact that he teaches the Gospel rightly. The Gospel has to be the *successio*."[4] The validity of the Church and her ministry are not bound to "the orderly succession of the bishops as popery pretends."[5] But Apostolic Succession in a real Christian sense can only be succession in those things "which the successors teach, command and order."[6] It is a succession in the Apostles' doctrine, work and spirit. Thus a power to ordain is given to those who do the Apostles' work and share their faith. *"Nos qui praedicamus euangelium habemus potestatem ordinandi"*[7] (We who preach the Gospel also have the power to ordain). "We who are assembled in the name of Christ, we also have the Word. If we should agree that this or that man should be ordained to the Ministry, he is certainly ordained."[8] Where there are the pure Word and Sacrament, there is the true Church, but where there is a true Church, there must also be all rights given to the Church including the

---

[1] *W.A.*, 19, 72; *Briefw.*, October 28th, 1525, and No. 1,036 (September 3rd, 1526?).
[2] *Briefw.*, November 17th, 1524; cf. de Wette, 6, 379f.
[3] *Briefw.*, December 12th, 1535; *W.A.* 38, 234ff.; exposition in full, *W.A.*, 39, II, 176ff.
[4] *W.A.*, 39, II, 177.   [5] *W.A.*, 21, 333, 32; cf. *W.A.* 39, I, 185, 5.
[6] *W.A.*, 39, I, 185ff.; cf. pp. 188ff.   [7] *Tischr.*, 4, 867.   [8] *W.A.*, 15, 721, 7.

right of ordaining ministers. "It would be incredible that *we* (the Lutherans after their separation from Rome) should have all the great gifts of the Church, God's Word, Christ, Spirit, faith, prayer, baptism, the Lord's Supper, the Keys, the ministry, and should *not* have the least of the Church's gifts and possessions—namely, the power to call some men to the ministry to administer all these gifts."[1]

As the validity of ordination requires the existence of the "pure" Gospel, so there follows a negative consequence: ministry and ordination are invalidated through the lack of the pure Gospel, through wrong doctrine.[2] For this reason many Lutheran Churches treated Roman Catholic ordination as invalid, being convinced that the Roman idea of priesthood was inseparably mixed up with very wrong doctrine. As far as I know, the general Lutheran practice is still to re-ordain Roman Catholic priests who seek admission to the Lutheran ministry. In Germany this has been the case several times in the last few decades and is expressly prescribed by the laws of some Lutheran Churches.

Luther objected to the whole Roman Catholic idea of priesthood and consecration, to the character of the Mass as a means of earning merit for the living or dead, linked up as it is with the wrong idea of Eucharistic sacrifice. He also objected to the celibacy of the clergy, to certain sacraments which were not founded on the Bible, to unbiblical ritual, etc. All this, in Luther's eyes, had turned the Christian ministry (*Ministerium*—namely, the service instituted by God in His Church) into popish priesthood (*Sacerdotium*—namely, priests bringing sacrifices to God and mediating between God and man like a *pontifex*, a bridge-builder between God and man). Luther thought that the Roman conception had also been formed to some extent on the model of the Old Testament priesthood, in spite of the fact that this priesthood no longer exists in the New Testament and Christian Church because Christ has been our High Priest once and for ever by His own sacrifice, and this sacrifice cannot be repeated. The laws governing the Roman priest's office, forcing him to recognise in teaching and practice all these wrong principles, made it quite impossible for a Roman priest to preach the Gospel purely and to administer the sacraments rightly. According to Luther, it can be taken for granted that the Roman priest, as a consequence of his priesthood, cannot stand in the proper Apostolic Succession, but is bound to

---

[1] *W.A.* 38, 252, 10ff.; cf. *Tischr.* 659; in Luther's opinion, this conception of Apostolic Succession prevailed in the New Testament and Early Church. *W.A.*, 38, 253; Schmalkald. art. quoted in *Bekenntnisschriften*, 430

[2] *W.A.*, 21, 507, 10; pp. 406; 426ff.; *W.A.*, 31, I, 208, 11; 33,306; 33, 454, 26; *Tischr.*, 4,395, 6,234.

be different from an Apostle or a Minister of the Gospel.[1] Therefore Luther publicly warns young men not to accept Roman Orders. These Orders would destroy the ordinand's conscience and could never make him a real minister of the Gospel.[2]

And yet Luther claims not to be a Donatist; he agrees that there may be hypocrites and morally bad people among the ministers of a church and that this would not invalidate the Church's functions and sacraments.[3] But the wrong doctrine would do so. The general doctrinal position of a minister must be in order, and no good Christian ought to take the sacraments from the hand of a minister who preaches the wrong doctrine on the sacraments.[4] For Luther, this applied to Roman Catholics, Zwinglians and Anabaptists in the same way.

In order to understand this attitude of Luther's, we have to realise that all his religious experience was concentrated on justification by faith alone. He had tried to proclaim this experience as a priest and university professor in the Roman Catholic Church; but he had failed. The Pope would not tolerate this doctrine and excommunicated him. It was obvious that the ordinary priest in village and town would have no better chance. His very priesthood under the Pope's jurisdiction prevented him from doing his duty, from leading people to "the Gospel." Therefore ordination to this priesthood could not transfer to the ordinands the ministry that preaches reconciliation.

This does not mean that the Lutherans re-ordained all priests who had been ordained under the old order in pre-Reformation days. Those priests who were not *only* ordained in order to say Mass for the living or dead, but who had been properly called to a preaching ministry or teaching office in church or university[5] were recognised without re-ordination if they were willing and able to continue their office in the spirit of "the Gospel." One could perhaps speak of a kind of re-examination. According to the

---

[1] For the whole passage, see *W.A.*, 6, 303ff.; 8, 484–563; 38, 195ff.; 41, 180f.; 53, 242ff.; *Tischr.*, 3,424; ordination of "Mass priests" who continually crucify Christ by re-enacting his death is satanic. *W.A.*, 54, 436f. and *ibid.*, pp. xl–xlii; Luther himself has crucified God during many years by saying Mass. *Tischr.*, 139; cf. 5,589.

[2] *W.A.*, 6, 566, 9; 12, 173ff.

[3] e.g. *Tischr.*, 342, 605; cf. Augsbg. Conf., Art. VIII.

[4] *W.A.*, 10, III, 173ff.; 397, 31; 21,507, 10; 28, 469ff.; *Tischr.*, 342, 574, 3,822, 5,184, 5,661; cf. Elert, *op. cit.*, I, 306f.; wrong doctrine invalidates the episcopal office. *W.A.*, 53, 233ff., esp. 242f.; if it is impossible to attend a Church where the Word is preached purely and the sacrament administered rightly, it is better to abstain from attending Church altogether, and the *desire* to receive the sacrament and absolution is sufficient in the eyes of God. *W.A.*, 7, 293ff.; 38, 88ff.; *Briefw.*, August 27th, 1532, April 11th, 1533.

[5] *W.A.*, 38, 236, 4.

THE CHURCH AS THE BODY OF CHRIST 77

plan of Luther and his friends, *visitatores* with knowledge in theology and Church law went through the parishes examining doctrine, gifts and morals of the priests. If they were satisfied, the priest could continue as Lutheran minister. Those priests, however, who were not able to preach the Gospel in the right way were dismissed.[1] One has to admit that the reports of these *visitatores* give a shocking impression of the intellectual and moral state of the pre-Reformation priest. No fairminded Christian can deny that some sort of reformation was necessary *in those days*, and one must not compare the priests of the pre-Reformation times with the much superior Roman Catholic priest of to-day.[2]

6. What is the ministry?

We have spoken a great deal of the ministry without stating the Lutheran conception of the ministry.

Who ought to preach the Word and who ought to administer the Sacraments? The official Lutheran answer was, from the very beginning: God has instituted a ministry, the office of individual persons, properly called and ordained for this purpose.[3]

Some think that Luther in his earlier years took a different line by emphasising the universal priesthood of all baptised believers. It is true that he proclaimed this doctrine mainly in the period between 1519 and 1523.[4] But even then this never led him to abolish the ministry. He gives various reasons for that. Theological knowledge, special training, and personal qualities are necessary.[5] The ministry is the property of the whole congregation and no one should take it upon himself without the consent of the whole congregation. The idea of the universal priesthood of all believers would therefore be misused if everybody were allowed to speak and preach in the Church.[6] This would be like the women's conversations in the market-place, everyone wanting to speak and no one to hear,[7] a turbulent chattering like the croaking of frogs.[8] And how disorderly it would be if all Christians wanted to

[1] Cf. *W.A.*, 26, 235; 30, III, 541ff., esp. 552, 32; *Briefw.*, November 30th, 1525; November 10th, 1531; March 25th, 1534; August 5th, 1539; September 19th, 1539.
[2] C. A. H. Burkhardt, *Geschichte der saechsischen Kirchen-und Schulvisitation*, Leipzig, 1879.
[3] Augsbg. Conf., Articles V, XIV.
[4] *W.A.*, 6, 370, 564, 582; 8, 273ff.; 11, 96, 24; 11, 411ff.; 12, 180ff.; 12, 309; 12, 522, 5. Luther based this doctrine on the following Biblical passages: 1 Cor. iv. 1; Gal. iii. 28; 1 Pet. ii. 9; Rev. i. 6, v. 10.
[5] *Tischr.*, 483, 626, 744, 2,473, 5,511, 6,000, 6,793; Knowledge of classical languages: *W.A.*, 30, II, 545ff., and *Tischr.*, 6,805.
[6] *W.A.*, 6, 407f., 564ff.; 8,495ff.; 10, III, 170ff., 395f.; 11, 412f. 12, 189, 21; 12, 308, 29; 25, 16, 23; 41, 204f.
[7] *W.A.*, 10, III, 397, 17.   [8] *W.A.*, 10, I (2), 239, 18.

baptise! A thousand hands would try to grasp the child, who would be drowned in the water.¹ But reading Luther's utterances before 1523 gives the impression that even then reasons of order and decency are not the only ones, but that deeper theological considerations are in his mind.

After 1524, the idea of the universal priesthood of all believers was no longer stressed in Luther's teaching. It almost disappears into the background and other considerations come into the open: God Himself has instituted the Ministry,² and it is by divine ordinance that the Church has to call specially appointed ministers.³

Many scholars think that a complete break in Luther's ideas took place. There is no doubt that his emphasis in the doctrine of the ministry altered very much in the years 1524–5. This may be explained by historical development. In the earlier years, when confronted with the Roman hierarchy, he emphasised the universal priesthood of all believers against the monopoly of the consecrated priest. In later years, when faced with the enthusiasts, Karlstadt, the Peasants' Revolution, with laymen preaching and claiming direct divine vocation and revelation, referred to a kind of inner life, he emphasises the contrary: God instituted the ministry, which, in ordinary circumstances, alone has the right of preaching and administering sacraments. But this latter conception could already be traced in his earlier years,⁴ while the idea of universal priesthood of all believers was never quite extinct from Luther's mind.⁵ He says: "It is true, we are all priests—but we are not all vicars (*Pfarrherr*)."⁶ Stressing this point, he occasionally re-introduces the old distinction between "clergy" and "laymen."⁷

Luther's opinion is well illustrated by the parable of the citizens and the mayor. All citizens have equal civic rights. But this does

---

¹ *W.A.*, 17, II, 452f.

² *W.A.*, 21, 421, 21; 28, 466–79; 30, II, 528f.; 34, I, 319, 5; *ibid.*, 318ff.; 41, 123, 34; 300, 20; 45, 461, 13; 46, 277, 3; 52, 566, 10.

³ It is important that the minister should be properly called by the Church: *W.A.*, 16, 33ff.; 17, II, 493, 14; 30, III, 510ff.; *Tischr.*, 90, 113, 483; Luther stresses the importance of divinity degrees as conferring a teaching office in the Church; he would have felt neither compelled nor entitled to carry out his work of reformation had it not been for his degree ("a sworn Doctor of Divinity"); e.g. *W.A.*, 31, I, 212, 6; *Tischr.*, 453; see above, p. 20, note 2; the fact should be noted that in Luther's time the universities were virtually a part of the Church; the Doctors of Wittenberg had to sign the Augsburg Confession.

⁴ *W.A.*, 6, 440, 21 (1520); *Der Fuss Christi ist das Prediger Amt*, *W.A.*, 8, 24, 13 (1521–2).

⁵ See below, p. 79, notes 3 and 5.

⁶ *W.A.*, 31, I, 211, 16.

⁷ *W.A.*, 30, III, 525, 19ff; 31, I, 211, 5.

THE CHURCH AS THE BODY OF CHRIST 79

not mean that every individual citizen may arbitrarily take upon himself the office of mayor. All citizens together elect one of their own community to be the mayor, who, in the name of all, has to administer the common rights of the city. He does not *become* a citizen by this election; he *is* already a citizen and brings his right as a citizen with him into the office of mayor.[1]

In the same way, all Christians have equal rights as priests, but they cannot arbitrarily take upon themselves the functions derived from this priesthood. They must elect one of their number to the "highest office in Christendom,"[2] i.e. they must delegate to him the power to administer the common rights of a Christian community. The Christian does not become a priest by election to the ministry or by ordination. He was already a priest by baptism.[3] *Nos omnes esse æqualiter sacerdotes, quotquot baptisati sumus.*[4] But his election as a minister bestows on him the right to exercise all priestly functions, i.e. the divinely instituted ministry. Because it is the will of God that these functions are reserved for the ministry only.

"For, praise God, in our churches we can present to a Christian a proper Christian Mass, as ordained and instituted by Christ and in accordance with Christ's and the Church's intention. At the altar stands our vicar, bishop or curate, rightly, properly and publicly called, previously consecrated by baptism, anointed and born to be Christ's priest."[5]

In his later years Luther makes a real effort to strengthen the authority of the ministry.[6] "God wills to give the Holy Spirit to those only who receive it through the word and ministry (*Predigtamt*)."[7] The word and the ministry are both ordained by God.[8] Indeed Luther goes so far as to say: " . . . the Church, which means the number of baptised and believing Christians who are under the care of one vicar (*Pfarrherr*)."[9] "The true Church is externally known by the fact that she calls and ordains bishops, vicars and preachers."[10] This means that a proper Church is known by good Christian pastors who administer the Word and

---

[1] *W.A.*, 6,408; 8,503; 41, 208.
[2] *W.A.*, 11, 415, 30.
[3] *W.A.*, 6, 582, 9; 12, 178ff. (the whole book); still in later years 24, 282, 6 and 18; 38, 227ff.; 230; 47, 189; 49, 197.
[4] *W.A.*, 6, 564, 6.
[5] *W.A.*, 38, 247, 12; cf. *Tischr.*, 5,428; *W.A.*, 6, 407; 7, 633.
[6] *W.A.*, 17, II, 192; 19, 233, 15; 38, 243, 29.
[7] *W.A.*, 17, II, 135, 20.
[8] *Os enim ministri os Christi et auris ministri auris Christi est*: *Tischr.*, 5,176; cf. 5,178.
[9] *W.A.*, 30, II, 421, 19; 425, 22.
[10] *W.A.*, 50, 632, 35ff.

Sacrament in the right way. This explains why the German Church conflict after 1933 had as its centre the question of training, examining and ordaining ministers.

And yet in spite of his high authority the Lutheran minister is essentially very different from the Roman Catholic priest.[1] I think there is a deep meaning in the fact that Lutheran Churches—while in some places retaining the title of "priest" (Scandinavia)—prefer to call their ministers "pastors." The metaphor of a pastor, a shepherd, shows exactly what is meant. The shepherd is not the mediator between the sheep and the grass, the sheep having direct access to the grass.[2] But the shepherd shows them the right way to the meadow and defends them against dangers.

Luther's doctrine on the universal priesthood of all believers is not confirmed by the Augsburg Confession. This Confession simply underlines the conception of the divine institution of the ministry. "In order that people may obtain this faith, God has ordained the ministry."[3]

In Luther's opinion, it was a matter of course that nobody should become a minister unless he felt himself called by God.[4] But our own feelings very often deceive us. For this reason the inner call does not entitle anybody to take upon himself ministerial functions unless this call is confirmed by men in authority. Luther speaks of a twofold vocation (*vocatio duplex*). My conviction that God really has called me to the ministry of his Church will be confirmed by the fact that God leads me to find *men* who will send me to take up this work. God would cause a congregation or a Church government to call and ordain me for this ministry and to give me a written document testifying to this fact.[5]

There is no general divine rule as to the procedure of this call given to a candidate for the ministry by his fellow Christians. It has to be done according to the valid Church constitution of the district concerned. There are Lutheran Churches who elect their ministers by a vote of the congregation; in other Churches the bishops, synods, universities, protectors (so-called patrons), the king as the first layman of the Church, or other authorities co-operate in appointing ministers; in many Churches there is a

---

[1] *W.A.*, 12, 173, 39; 12, 180, 21; 38, 220ff.

[2] The priest cannot "make" the sacrament by his consecrating bread and wine; it is "made" by Christ Himself and only distributed by the priest. *W.A.*, 38, 239f.; *nos certe docemus panem et vinum esse corpus et sanguinem Christi, non consecrante ministro, sed sic volente per institutionem suam Christo. Briefw.*, November 27th, 1535; cf. *Tischr.*, 659.

[3] Augsbg. Conf., Art. V.

[4] *Tischr.*, 534; cf. 228, 453.

[5] See above, p 78, note 3, and *W.A.*, 28, 473, 35ff.; for the whole, *W.A.*, 30, III. 518ff.

system combining some or all of these factors. The decisive point is that those who have the legal and constitutional right of acting in the name of a particular congregation—whoever this may be— are calling the man to the ministry. "We teach concerning the government of the Church that no one ought to teach or preach publicly in the Church, or administer the Sacraments, without being duly called."[1]

7. *Ordination*

The call to the ministry is publicly confirmed by ordination. This ordination follows old Biblical models, but the details of the ceremony are not prescribed by God. For Luther, ordination is no sacrament. *Ordinare est vocare*, i.e. the call to the ministry is the most important part in connection with the ordination.[2] This means that, on the one hand, ordination is a public confirmation on the part of the legal Church authorities (or neighbouring vicars) that the ordinand has been called to the ministry in legal form.

On the other hand, ordination is a public declaration by responsible Church authorities to the effect that the ordinand is supposed to preach the pure Gospel and to be a real successor to the Apostles. For this reason, Lutheran ordination was always connected with examination. This examination is essentially a Church act. The Church may accept university degrees as part of this examination, but it must reserve the ultimate right to accept or reject a candidate for ordination. A merely academic degree of an interdenominational university would not be sufficient, nor would a State examination suffice, because the admission to the ministry does not only depend on knowledge and scholarship, but on the doctrine and ecclesiastical qualifications of the candidate. Purely Lutheran faculties like the one in Wittenberg, however, might act as the examination board of the Church, but not an interdenominational faculty.

By accepting the ministry, the candidate accepts certain obligations. The order of ordination used by the Lutherans in the early days makes the ordaining minister charge the candidate that it is his duty to preach the pure Gospel. Some years later, a formal vow was required from the candidate that he would preach the Gospel purely and reject all heretical doctrine. Still later, this point was defined in a stricter sense by requiring a vow from the candidates (or a vow *and* a signature) pledging the candidate to

---

[1] Augsbg. Conf., Art. XIV.

[2] *W.A.*, 15, 721; 38, pp. 195ff., 231, 236ff., 401ff.; 50, 632, 35; *Briefw.*, No. 2,242; *Bekenntnisschriften*, p. 458, note 2.

exercise his ministry according to the principles laid down in the Bible and interpreted by the Augsburg Confession.[1]

The ministry is, on the one hand, the office of the whole Church, and therefore the ministers are ordained once in their lives by a responsible member of the Church administration in one of the most important Churches of the country. Thus, the Parish Church of Wittenberg was used as a centre for ordination from 1535 and the Vicar (Bugenhagen), and Luther himself ordained there ministers of Lutheran Churches in many countries.[2] In later years, the other Lutheran Churches established ordination centres of their own and Wittenberg became more and more the place of ordination for Saxony only.[3]

But, on the other hand, the minister is ordained for a particular parish, he is not just consecrated in order to be a priest, to belong to a special privileged class of clergy, or to receive special powers. It is not even sufficient to hold a formal title which does not involve preaching and administering the Sacraments. For the minister is ordained to do this special task; he is not ordained to a priesthood, a *sacerdotium*, but to a ministry, a *ministerium*, a special kind of service.

On the one hand, the pastor is ordained as the minister of the whole church, on the other hand, as the minister of a particular congregation. For this reason, the "central" ordination by which the minister is ordained once in his lifetime (at Wittenberg or some other ecclesiastical centre) is followed by a local induction of the ordained minister into his particular congregation. Luther has not fixed an exact theory of the relation between ordination and induction. During the early years of the Reformation he seems to think that both acts might be merged into one, but later he distinguishes between them. An indication of his opinion is contained in a letter to the Vicar of Gotha. The congregation at Gotha elected a curate and sent him to Wittenberg for examination and ordination. Luther wrote to the Vicar:

> "We are sending back your John called and elected by you, and also examined and publicly ordained and confirmed into your curacy by us before our congregation (church) with prayers to, and praises of God."[4]

---

[1] P. Drews, *Die Ordination, Prüfung und Lehrverpflichtung* (*op. cit.*); G. Rietschel, *Lehrbuch der Liturgik* (*op. cit.*), II, 427ff.; Elert, *op. cit.*, I, 303ff.; a bishop's vow at his induction (consecration), *W.A.*, 53, 224, note 1.

[2] Luther ordains ministers for another country, *W.A.*, 54, 488, 8; *Briefw.*, April 22nd, 1539; July 27th, 1539; August 12th, 1539.

[3] G. Rietschel, *op. cit.*, II, 418ff.; *W.A.*, 34, I, 437, 16; cf. Adolf Scholz, *Bugenhagens Kirchenordnungen in ihrem Verhältnis zueinander*, Diss. 1913, pp. 34, 37f. H. Asmussen, *Die Kirche und das Amt*, München, 1939, pp. 283f.

[4] *Briefw.*, October 20th, 1535.

It is an interesting theoretical problem whether a Lutheran minister could be ordained by laymen. The younger Luther was inclined to admit this in cases of emergency. If a number of believing and baptised Christians were to find themselves shipwrecked on an island, and if there were one among them fit to preach and act as pastor, they could elect and ordain him to the ministry by themselves and he would even have the right to administer Sacraments to these people.[1] For the believing congregation possesses the "Apostolic Succession."

The rule, however, is, that the existing ministers ought to pass on the ministry to the next generation. "*Sed nos qui iam habemus ministeria, commendabimus in nostrum ministerium.*"[2] Ministers are ordained by ministers, the congregation exercising its functions by co-operating in the election only.

The ordination does not give to the minister a *character indelebilis*. The rights given through ordination may be revoked,[3] but not without reason and only by the lawful authority of the Church concerned. The only lawful reasons are heresy, immorality, and lack of gifts (e.g., if the minister becomes mentally incapacitated). But there must be a proper hearing and trial. The rights of ordination cannot be cancelled arbitrarily by a bishop or by a majority vote of a congregation or Church assembly without proper reasons.[4] Church authorities whose members themselves have become heretic or immoral have no right to take from a minister the powers granted him by ordination. Luther illustrates his ideas by referring to his office as a doctor of divinity and lecturer in the University. He said these rights were bestowed upon him under the existing constitution by Emperor and Pope. Both would now like to revoke these rights and to stop his preaching and teaching, but they could not do so because they were heretics themselves, and had lost their right to speak for the Church.[5] When the citizens and magistrates of Zwickau dismissed one minister for immorality and other reasons, Luther did not recognise their decision, as no proper Church authority had been consulted. He was extremely furious at the attempts of secular authorities to interfere with the freedom of the ministry and

---

[1] *W.A.*, 6, 407f.; cf. p. 440; 11, 413f.; 12, 193, 37ff.

[2] *W.A.*, 15, 721, 1ff.; cf. *W.A.*, 53, 257.

[3] *W.A.*, 6, 408, 17; 6, 567, 18; 12, 309, 9; 15, 721, 13; *Tischr.*, 829.

[4] *Briefw.*, November 30th, 1525; April 3rd, 1531; March 25th, 1534; *W.A.*, 6, 440ff.; 17, II, 232; 21, 205, 14; Ministers whose morals are questioned, but who otherwise do their duty, are treated fairly leniently by Luther if they promise to improve their moral conduct. He knows that sin can *really* be forgiven in the Church. *Heresy* is a much greater crime in Luther's eyes.

[5] *W.A.*, 31, I, 212, 6.

opened a most violent campaign against "the beasts of Zwickau."[1] When, after 1933, Nazi State authorities or nazified bishops or Church authorities tried to take away the ministerial rights from such Christian ministers as remained loyal to their convictions, the reply was made that they themselves were heretics and un-Christian people, and that this fact alone made it impossible for them to be able to interfere with the ministry of others, and that on principle no minister could be deprived of his rights arbitrarily without proper proceedings.

8. *Validity of Lay celebrations*

In fact, Lutheranism always emphasised the great value of a proper ordination. In Lutheran Church law there is a great difference between a non-ordained candidate and an ordained minister.[2] If a man who is not ordained acts as if he were a minister (celebrating the Sacraments, hearing confession and pronouncing absolution, etc.) it is deemed to be a great sin before God. But it would not be "invalid." We could almost compare it with a man who drives a railway engine without a licence. This would be a grave offence, yet the train would move "illegally" but "validly." Such procedure could only be justified in cases of emergency. Nobody would reproach an unlicensed engine-driver for saving a train by driving the engine in the case of a particular emergency. But if the same man wanted to become a regular engine-driver he would have to take his examination and acquire a licence. In the same way shipwrecked Christians might call and ordain somebody to act as their minister; his Word and Sacrament would be perfectly valid,[3] but if he were taken back to Christian countries and wished to become an ordinary minister, his ordination would have to be confirmed and recognised by some special act of the Church whose minister he wanted to become.

Luther fails to understand why ministerial acts by laymen should be invalid. He always emphasises that Word and sacraments must not be separated. Now, even the Catholics cannot deny that a sermon preached by a layman may convert a person and that a layman's baptism is valid. But in Catholic view, a layman cannot celebrate the Lord's Supper and pronounce the absolution validly. Luther thinks this is a hair-splitting distinction, declaring

---

[1] *W.A.*, 34, I, 549, 16; 34, II, 573; allusions, *ibid.*, pp. 75ff.; *Briefw.*, Nos. 1,788, 1,789, 1,790, 1,792, 1,801, 1,802, 1,804, 1,806, 1,807, 1,854, 1,855, 1,881, 1,917; cf. Köstlin-Kawerau, *Martin Luther, sein Leben und seine Schriften, Fünfte neubearbeitete Auflage*, Berlin, 1903, II, 270ff.; McKinnon, *op. cit.*, IV, pp. 77–80.

[2] F. Heiler, *Im Ringen um die Kirche*, München, 1931, p. 454.

[3] Emergency cases: *W.A.*, 11, 412, 16; 12, 171f.; 12, 189, 26; *Tischr.*, 6,672.

the Word and one sacrament to be valid if administered by a layman, while declaring the absolution and the second sacrament under similar circumstances to be invalid. This subdivision is quite unacceptable to Luther.[1] Also the present-day distinction between a "valid" and an "effective" sacrament[2] is alien to Luther's mind. If a sacrament is effective it is also valid. What else should "valid" mean than that "it achieves its purpose"?

When Christ said to His disciples in the night in which He was betrayed, "Take, eat, this is my Body," and "Do this in remembrance of me," He does not make any difference between those who eat the Sacrament and those who distribute it. Either the Catholic interpretation is right, i.e. the Apostles and their successors (consecrated bishops and priests) were exclusively asked to administer the Sacrament, in which case only they were asked to receive it. Or, laymen also may receive it—but in that case laymen also could administer it.[3] Therefore a lay administration is not invalid, but it is illegal, and is strictly forbidden except in the case of an emergency.[4] For God Himself instituted the ministry and this institution must not be despised. In later years Luther is inclined to forbid laymen to exercise any pastoral functions even in emergency cases.[5] Scared by disorders and religious fanatics, he would have liked to reserve all kinds of preaching, the conduct of services, and the administration of sacraments, to ordained ministers only.

9. *No degrees of the ministry—iure divino*

What about the subdivision of the ministry into bishop, priest and deacon? Luther thinks that there is definite proof in the New Testament and the writings of the early Church that the titles "bishop" and "priest" originally meant more or less one and the same office. Many scholars, including some Anglicans, admit this fact;[6] others doubt it or refer to tradition as the source of Church law. While Luther does not wish to destroy all tradition, he does not consider tradition to be vital. As bishops and priests are the same in the New Testament, it is, to say the least, not necessary and vital to have a distinction between them in our Churches. He himself, and still more his friend Melanchthon and others, are inclined to maintain the three degrees of the Ministry for practical

---

[1] *W.A.*, 6,408, 1; 10, III, 395; 11, 415, 30; 12, 181, 11; 12, 522, 5ff.; *Tischr.*, 659.
[2] L. Hodgson, *The Second World Conference on Faith and Order*, held at Edinburgh, 1937, London, 1938, pp. 241ff.
[3] *W.A.*, 12, 180, 34; cf. 6, 563, 10.   [4] *W.A.*, 17, II, 192.   [5] *Tischr.*, 6,361.
[6] A. C. Headlam, *op. cit.*, pp. 97ff.

reasons as a good tradition created by man, provided this subdivision worked well. In fact, it did not. The majority of bishops persecuted those persons who preached the Gospel as Luther understood it. Luther was faced with the alternative of either retaining a Church with episcopacy—but, as he thought, with the wrong doctrine—or establishing a Church with pure doctrine, but without episcopacy. He does not waver in his choice. For him episcopacy is not necessary for true Apostolic Succession or valid ordination; pure doctrine, however, is. He has to drop the less essential episcopacy in order to retain the essentials of the Church —namely, the validity of the Word, the sacraments and the ministry.[1]

Luther puts his opinion very clearly in his official statement about ordination: *"if the bishops were real bishops who served the Church and the Gospel, we could, for the sake of peace and unity in the Church, permit them to ordain and confirm our ministers, but not as though it were a matter of necessity. And they should omit all masks and phantoms of unchristian pomp and ritual.*

"Now, as they are not real bishops nor wish to be, but secularised Lords and Princes . . . persecuting and condemning those who are properly called to the ministry, the Church has no need to remain without ministers because the bishops refuse to co-operate.

"Therefore, according to the example of the Early Church and Early Fathers, we ourselves have to ordain suitable persons to this ministry. And they [the bishops] are not able to prevent us from doing so, not even according to their own church law. For their law says that even those who are ordained by heretics are ordained validly."[2]

To those who claim that an "Apostolic Succession by Ordination" was necessary for the validity of the ministry, Luther would say that even this condition was fulfilled among the Lutherans, as ordination to the Lutheran ministry was administered by priests. For him a "priestly succession" is completely sufficient for a valid ministry. Luther does not see any Biblical reason to distinguish between a *full* ministry of a bishop and a somewhat *limited* ministry of a priest. All those who are called or ordained to the ministry receive the full episcopal rights that God has bestowed upon the ministry. Luther does not see how it can be proved from the Scriptures that a priest may celebrate the Eucharist, but is not allowed to administer ordination and confirmation.[3] Where is the Biblical proof for thus distinguishing

[1] W.A., 30, II, 340ff.; 38, 195, 17f.; 38, 236, 23; 41, 241, 1; *Briefw.*, No. 1,822; *Tischr.*, 4,595; *Bekenntnisschriften*, p. 457.
[2] Schmalk. Art. pars III, X; see *Bekenntnisschriften*, p. 457f.
[3] The Biblical terms "priest" and "bishop" signify the same office, e.g. Acts xx. 17f. (*W.A.*, 25, 17, 7); Titus i. 5–7 (*W.A.*, 8, 500, 19); 1 Pet. v. 1 (*W.A.*, 10, II, 144, 25); cf. *W.A.*, 6, 429, 15; 6, 440, 21; 10, II, 112ff.; 12, 287; *Tischr.*, 5,272;

between the office of a full bishop on the one hand, and, on the other hand, of a half-bishop who is called priest and possesses only part of the episcopal rights?[1]

Thus the ordination of almost all German, Danish and Norwegian Lutheran ministers, superintendents and bishops can be traced back to two priests—namely, to Luther himself and to his friend Bugenhagen, the Vicar of Wittenberg.[2] In Sweden and Finland, the episcopal ordination and succession were retained by an accident of history.

10. *An episcopacy—iure humano*[3]

Thus, on principle, all priests are bishops. And yet Luther recognised that the individual priest or pastor ought not to have ultimate authority in the Church. The Church would have to think out some way of controlling the doctrine and work of the individual pastors, and the training, examination and lawful vocation and ordination of candidates for the ministry. As no details are prescribed by God, the Church must try by all means to find out the most suitable form of organisation. This organisation may change at various times and in various countries according to changing conditions. This authority for controlling the doctrine and ministers in a diocese can be given to a body of Christians, a committee of ministers and laymen (a *Consistorium*—Church *collegium*), e.g. a Lutheran university faculty, a council of vicars (*Geistliches Ministerium, Hauptpastoren-Collegium*) or even a kind of super-minister, a *pastor pastorum*. He would be a minister whose congregation consists of the ministers of a diocese. His relation to the ministers of the diocese is roughly the same as that of a vicar to his flock; roughly speaking—because things are, of course, slightly different. The super-minister has the task of controlling and encouraging the continuous studies of his ministers, and thus

---

"*Est ergo notandum, quod Pauli ordinatio fuit, ut per civitates singulas presbyteros in plurali numero eligat, et vocantur episcopi, seniores. Ergo tempore apostolorum habuit unaquaeque civitas plures episcopos* . . . [after speaking about the 'abuses']. *Unaquaeque civitas debet multos habere Episcopos i.e. inspectores et visitatores . . . Nos apostolico ritu vocamur sumusque episcopi.*" W.A., 25, 16, 25; 17, 2 and 13; for the whole passage, pp. 16ff. W.A., 38, 237f.; Tischr., 3,829; cf. Holl, op. cit., pp. 353, 357.

[1] Luther tries to prove that the Early Church knew a non-episcopal ordination. W.A., 30, II, 335, 15; 38, 238, 1; Bekenntnisschriften, 430, 458. This opinion is partly justified by F. Heiler, op. cit., pp. 479–516; cf. H. Asmussen, *Die Kirche und das Amt* (op. cit.), pp. 199ff.

[2] The value of this "priestly succession" recognised by F. Heiler, ibid., pp. 456f., 497.

[3] H. H. Kramm, *The "Pastor Pastorum" in Luther and Early Lutheranism* in *And Other Pastors of Thy Flock*, op. cit., Cambridge 1942, pp. 124–134.

supervising the way they do their work, but he has also to be their pastor, strengthening and consoling them, hearing their confession and giving them absolution, and he has to examine and ordain candidates for the ministry; sometimes he even controls their training.[1] The exact title of this *pastor pastorum* is a matter of taste and does not matter very much. Many Lutheran Churches retained or reintroduced the old title "bishop." Luther himself preferred the title bishop, but he did not oppose the ugly Latin translation—"superintendent," which was used in his own country.[2] There is a real museum of titles for the *pastor pastorum* in Lutheran churches, e.g. *General-superintendent, Landes-superintendent, Oberhofprediger, Senior, Landesbischof.*

But we must never forget that *in essence* and *by ordination* a Lutheran bishop is not different from other ministers: he is only a minister with a special kind of work. Luther did not want to abolish the ministerial degree of episcopacy; he considered all vicars to be bishops, abolishing the lower degree of limited bishop called "priest," and the still more limited bishop called "deacon."[3]

Therefore for Luther it was a matter of sober and serious human deliberation whether or not he ought to favour episcopal church constitutions. He decides the question in each territory as each case arises according to the conditions prevailing in that special area. Where the bishop accepted the Gospel, Luther liked him to remain in office (e.g. in the present East Prussia which for some decades after the Reformation had a Church with "consecrated" Lutheran bishops). Luther clearly indicates that he does not wish to abolish episcopacy, but to reform it.[4] Originally, he even hoped to save the episcopal constitution for the whole of Germany under a Primate, the Archbishop of Mainz, whom he expected to become the head of an independent Episcopal German Church.[5] If this plan had been successful, the constitution of the German Lutheran Church would have developed on lines rather similar to the Church of England. The refusal of the Primate and

---

[1] He has to rule them by "the Word," and a Lutheran minister is bound to disobey his bishop if the latter's orders are incompatible with the Word of God; for such an attitude invalidates the bishop's office. W.A., 53, 220ff.; Augsbg. Conf., Art. XXVIII; Pastor Niemoeller and the other German pastors of the "Confessional Church" based their duty to disobey the "German Christian" bishops expressly on this article; similar arguments can be found in the Norwegian Church conflict against the Quisling-appointed bishops.

[2] He likes, however, to call the superintendents "bishops." Tischr., 4,717, 5,283.

[3] Cf. W.A., 53, 257, 15.

[4] *Me non optare ruinam Episcopatuum, sed reformationem. Briefw.*, May 20th, 1539; cf. W.A., 53, 219ff.; 223f.; 254, 8; Tischr., 3,829, 4,358, 4,595, 4,731.

[5] W.A., 6, 429ff.

most of the Bishops made this development impossible.[1] Therefore in the territories where the Bishops resisted the Reformation, different types of Church constitution developed. In Luther's own country the episcopal rights were shared between the theological faculty of Wittenberg, superintendents, the Prince and a *consistorium*. Under his advice and control, various constitutions were introduced, most of them with the help of his friend Bugenhagen, who re-organised the Churches in North Germany, Denmark and Norway. In important cities Bugenhagen transferred the spiritual episcopal rights to a council of vicars under the chairmanship of a superintendent. In Denmark and Norway he retained an episcopal constitution. The titles "bishop" and "superintendent" were used side by side for some time, the former prevailing. In his later years Luther himself also favoured the organisation of the Church under Lutheran bishops.[2] He himself consecrated the new Bishops of Naumburg and Merseburg. He saw no reason why he should not himself ordain these bishops as he was a priest and held the pure doctrine.[3] Apparently he did not seriously try to persuade a "consecrated" bishop to act as ordinator.[4] The belief held in some circles that Luther only very reluctantly abolished the episcopal consecration because he could find no bishop to take part in these ordinations seems to me unconvincing.[5] I have reason to believe that he would have got such bishops (Brandenburg, Prussia, Sweden, Finland, and some suffragan bishops) if he really had tried. I personally have found no indication that he made any serious effort. Melanchthon and some other Lutherans deplored the dying out of the old episcopal order more than did Luther and Bugenhagen.

As previously mentioned, Sweden and Finland kept the "Episcopal Succession," but Finland replaced it by a "Priestly Succession" in the nineteenth century as, all the bishops having died in the same year, the Russian Government refused permission for consecration of the new Finnish bishops by a foreign Lutheran bishop. This emergency resulted in the consecration of the new bishops by a priest. In recent times, certain Finnish and Baltic bishops were ordained with the assistance of the Swedish Archbishop, thus recovering the "Episcopal Succession."

[1] As late as 1530, Luther tried to win the Archbishop of Mainz for this plan. *W.A.*, 30 II, 391ff.; cf. *W.A.*, 18, 402ff.
[2] Holl, *op. cit.*, pp. 375ff.
[3] *W.A.*, 49, XXVI–XXIX; *W.A.*, 53, 219ff.; literature, *ibid.*, Luther as consecrator was assisted by three "superintendents" who were themselves consecrated priests. He claims that this kind of ordination of the Bishop of Naumburg is valid according to Catholic Church principles. *W.A.*, 53, 257.
[4] For the whole, O. Andersen, *Superintendentembedet* (*op. cit.*).
[5] W. Staehlin, *Vom göttlichen Geheimnis*, Kassel, 1936, pp. 101f.

For present-day discussion, it should be noted that a number of German Lutherans discussed the desirability of appointing bishops for their Churches. Some Churches, during the last twenty years, have had bishops (e.g. Hanover, Bavaria, Wurtenberg, Saxony and others). Opinion with regard to the usefulness of an Episcopal constitution is very divided among German Lutherans in these days. Many quote the good old Church tradition in favour of Episcopacy and are, more or less, satisfied with the actions of the bishops during the recent Church conflicts (Bishop Wurm of Wurtenberg, Bishop Berggrav of Norway, etc.). Others think that the dangers involved in Episcopacy (dictatorship in Church affairs) were so great, and its shortcomings during recent years so manifold, that other forms of Church constitutions ought to be preferred.

But not even all Lutherans who are in favour of bishops wish them to be consecrated in an "Episcopal Succession." It is true, there are many who emphasise that the traditional episcopal consecration is a good, useful Church order which the Lutheran Church ought not to give up without adequate reasons. Others very strongly dislike this view, and the emphasis on Episcopacy in the Church of England and in modern reunion movements has convinced them of the danger inherent in the system. This opinion is reflected in many parts of American Lutherism, as shown by the tone of the following quotation:

> "The Catholic view that ordination is a sacrament instituted by Christ imparting the Holy Spirit, the power of forgiving sins by the right of the priesthood and of effecting the sacrament and the character *indelebilis*, deals with myths throughout . . . the doctrine of the Catholic and Episcopalian Churches that the episcopal ordination by virtue of the Apostolic Succession confers 'holy orders' deals with two additional myths. The 'holy order' of sacerdotalism does not exist, and there are no bishops *iure divino*. Furthermore, Ananias, who 'put his hand on Paul,' was neither an apostle nor a 'bishop,' Acts ix. 17. And they who performed the ceremony of the laying on of hands in the case of Timothy were simple presbyters, elders, pastors, 1 Tim. iv. 14."[1]

A similar attitude is revealed in the words of the Norwegian Professor E. Molland:

> "We [some Scandinavian Churches] have the succession as though we possessed it not . . . In our eyes it is, I should

[1] *Popular Symbolics* (*op. cit.*), pp. 109ff.

almost say, unworthy of the ministers of Christ to make the possession of the apostolic succession a condition for intercommunion."[1]

11. *Church constitutions, ceremonies and the Word of God*

There are two basic misconceptions about Luther's real attitude.[2] The first is that Luther's wish to base a Church on the Bible alone and to go back to the Apostles' time means that he does not only want to re-establish Apostolic doctrine, but also to reintroduce the constitution of the New Testament congregations and the order of service and liturgical dress of the Apostles (if any); the other misconception is that Luther did not care at all about matters of Church order or ceremonies, and allowed the Christians, or, still worse, the State, to decide these matters arbitrarily.

We have already seen (pp. 73f.) that these views are not correct. For Luther there is a *certain* connection between the Word of God on the one hand, and ceremonies on the other.

Certain elements of constitution and ritual are definitely *forbidden* by the letter or the spirit of the Word of God.[3] Such forbidden things are: the rule of the Pope in matters of conscience, the celibacy of the clergy, the customary form of monastic life, and, finally, the central core of the Roman liturgy, the eucharistic sacrifice in the Mass.[4] This last has produced misuse after misuse, like *cauda draconis*, a dragon's tail;[5] all these misuses had to be got rid of, including certain prayers in the canon of the Mass, Masses for the dead, for guilds and corporations, and all the other consequences of this practice. Neither could processions headed by the consecrated host be justified according to the Bible.

On the other hand, there were elements of constitution and ritual definitely *demanded* by the Bible; buildings must be provided where people could assemble to attend public worship and to listen to sermons.[6] In these buildings altars or Communion tables must be set up, where people can receive the Sacrament, and arrangements must be made for baptism.[7] Luther liked to quote the passage that God is not the author of confusion, but of order,

---

[1] E. Molland, "The Possibility of a United Christendom from the Scandinavian Standpoint," in *Union of Christendom*, ed. K. Mackenzie, London, 1938, p. 445.
[2] For the whole, cf. Elert, *op. cit.*, I, 280ff.; L. Fendt, *Der lutherische Gottesdienst des 16. Jahrhunderts*, München, 1923.
[3] *Briefw.*, March 14th, 1528; *W.A.*, 38, 584, 28.
[4] *Briefw.*, No. 1,822.
[5] Schmalk. art., *Bekenntnisschriften*, pp. 419ff.
[6] *W.A.*, 49, 588.
[7] *Briefw.*, No. 1,239.

and this Biblical principle demands a certain kind of order for the public services.[1] And it is the main task of the Church to arrange for the proper training, examination and appointment of ministers fit to administer the Word and the Sacrament. All this is definitely demanded through the letter and spirit of the Word of God.

In between the forbidden elements of constitution and ritual and those definitely prescribed there is a wide sphere of freedom.[2] But this freedom ought not to be used arbitrarily. As in a war the ultimate aim is fixed but the details of strategy are left to the High Command, so the ultimate aim of all Church order is fixed, the details, however, are entrusted to responsible and serious consideration on the part of experts. To give a few examples: no special form of university or theological college is prescribed in the Bible. It is, however, demanded in the New Testament that the minister responsible for a Christian congregation must have sufficient knowledge and experience for his task. No special form of examination is prescribed in Scripture, but it is demanded therein that the spirit and the gifts of a Christian are to be tested by the Church before he is admitted to a responsible office. No special kind of confirmation or ordination is demanded in the New Testament, but it is demanded that the Church should find orderly ways to govern the admission to the sacraments and to the ministry.[3]

There is a great amount of freedom, but there is a definite limitation to this freedom. It is governed and limited by the ultimate aim. This means that all Church laws or ceremonies which contradict the Bible and are detrimental to the Gospel must be abolished. This principle of Luther was one of the main arguments of the German Confessional Church in its resistance to State dictatorship in Church affairs after 1933. The State always claimed that it only interfered with the external constitution of the Church and that, according to Luther, all these external things of organisation did not matter for the conscience of the Christian and could be ruled by State law. The Church was subject to the dictatorship of State officials; a former bailiff was appointed

---

[1] *Nam reliquos ritus, una cum vestibus et altaribus et vasis, non video cur mutemus, cum in his pius esse possit usus, et absque ceremoniis vivi in ecclesia dei non possit.* Briefw., No. 679 (October, 1523, to Nicolaus Hausmann); cf. W.A., 12, 214, 14.

[2] Luther's distinction between obligatory, non-obligatory and forbidden ceremonies, etc., cf. W.A., 6, 447, 5; 10, III, 5ff.; 21ff., "*si velint*"; 12, 194, 15.

[3] No uniformity of Mass ritual is necessary, but some kind of Mass liturgy *must* exist. (*Briefw.*, May 21st, 1529), and the words of the consecration *must* be said, and all hosts and wine to be used *must* be properly consecrated. Luther urges the expulsion from Naumburg Diocese of a minister who had dropped the "consecrated" host, distributed instead an unconsecrated one, and had said that there was no difference between consecrated and unconsecrated hosts. *Tischr.*, 6,771.

president of the Saxonian Church and conquered the Church House in Dresden with the aid of a gun; storm-troop leaders who had resigned from Church membership were appointed to administer the Church finances, and the attempt was made to introduce racial laws into the Church, according to which Christians of Jewish origin, like St. Peter and St. Paul, or of half-Jewish origin, like St. Timothy, would no longer be allowed to write pastoral letters, nor even to fill the smallest Church office or hand the collection plate. On the other hand, the State protected ministers who baptised in the name of the German nation, who celebrated the Lord's Supper as a symbol of German blood and soil, and who took from the candidates for confirmation a vow, asking them: "Are you ready throughout your life to fight against Rome and against Judah? If so, then answer: Yes, so help me God."[1]

But against all Christian protests the State claimed that its activities were *only* designed to cover the sphere of *external* Church order, that the Church ought to be tolerant in doctrinal and liturgical matters, and that it was a deliberate lie of the Church opposition to accuse the State of interfering in religious beliefs. I mention this, not as a piece of political propaganda, but in order to show that there is definitely a very close connection between questions of Church order on the one side, and Biblical doctrine on the other. The German and Norwegian Lutheran Churches have learnt this lesson afresh. There is no need to define this connection in carefully formulated terms; any reasonable man will understand what Luther's conception means: freedom in detail, but subject to the ultimate aim of promoting the Gospel in word and action.

Adiaphora is the term by which the Lutherans described those elements of ritual and Church constitution which are neither demanded nor forbidden by Scripture (*adiaphora*: they make no difference). They are, therefore, examined by Luther under the categories of whether they are desirable or dangerous. Among things *desirable* is the ecclesiastical year with fixed Bible lessons for the Sundays, whereby the congregation is reminded again and again of the main doctrinal content of their faith in an orderly sequence covering the whole year. Desirable also are dignified ceremonies, which edify the congregation so long as they are simple and understandable. Desirable also is the use of the organ and of congregational singing as a method of prayer and adoration. It is good that the minister should wear special robes or vestments indicating that he is acting not as a private person. Certain beauty of Church buildings with their altars and pictures is good

[1] D. F. Buxton, *Christendom on Trial* (Friends of Europe), London, 1939, p. 24.

and uplifting for the congregation. Luther strenuously opposed their destruction by fanatical super-Protestants.[1]

Dangerous, on the other hand, was the reservation of the wine for the communicating priest only.[2] This was disobedience to the clear commandment of God and was bound to give an undue emphasis to the position of the priest. Dangerous also was the use of incense, and the blessing in church of such secular things as candles, foodstuffs, oil and consecrated altar stones. Of course, candles and altar stones could be used for divine worship, but there was no Biblical demand to consecrate them.

In these matters Luther was always very anxious "not to pour out the baby with the bath water." He does not abolish the customary mass ceremony, but his aim is to purify and reform it.[3] He shows the same attitude towards episcopacy, priesthood, etc. And when the Provost of Berlin asked him whether, without damaging his conscience, he could yield to the Elector's wish to keep certain ceremonies, Luther replied that he would not mind if the Provost wore three Mass vestments, one on top of the other, if one was not sufficient for him, and went seven times round the church in procession, as long as the Word of God were preached purely in Berlin and as long as there was no superstitious use of the ceremonies.[4]

This latter limitation is very typical of Luther.[5] Church laws and ceremonies which had for a long time worked to the advantage of the Church may through misuse become intolerable and have to be abolished.[6] For instance, if a bad Prime Minister were to use his right of influencing episcopal appointments in the established Church to provide the Church with pagan bishops, the order for the election of bishops, good as it may have been for centuries, must be abolished and disobeyed. For it no longer works for the benefit of the Church. This principle had a recent application in Norway, where a certain co-operation between the

---

[1] *Briefw.*, April 2nd, 1530; January 11, 1531; *Tischr.*, 867; *W.A.*, 15, 334ff.; 19, 99, 17; 26, 222f.; 231, 26; 28, 678; 30, III, 191, 35. "*Et licet ceremoniae necessariae non sunt ad salutem, tamen vulgo quaedam prosunt ad movendos stupidos animos. Dico autem potissimum de missarum ceremoniis, quales sunt altaria, vestes, candelae, et huiusmodi leviculae. . . .*" *Briefw.*, No. 1,768. "*Anhaldenses retinent multas ceremonias. Cum Lutherus haec audisset, dixit se cum voluptate ea omnia audivisse, und sie sollten also dies behalten.*" *Tischr.*, 7,131 (appendix in *W.A.*, 48, 693, 13).

[2] e.g. *W.A.*, 38, 88ff.; *Briefw.*, March 17th, 1531; August 27th, 1532; April 11, 1533.

[3] Schmalk. art., *Bekenntnisschriften*, 419; *W.A.*, 10, III, 1ff.; 12, 205ff.; 18, 62ff., esp. 123; 19, 14ff., esp. 72ff.

[4] *Briefw.*, December 4th, 1539 (No. 3,421).

[5] *Tischr.*, 4,761; 5,589; *W.A.*, 10, III, 14, 16f.; 38, 228, 33f.; *Bekenntnisschriften,* p. 419.

[6] *W.A.*, 19, 113.

State and the Church in appointing bishops, which had worked satisfactorily for centuries, had become intolerable. It was quite in accordance with Luther's doctrine if the majority of Norwegian Lutheran pastors obeyed God rather than men and refused allegiance to those new bishops who were appointed under State pressure by Quisling authorities.

From the foregoing it becomes clear that Luther does not use the Bible as a binding law book in matters of Church order, nor does he try to justify or prove every detail of Church organisation from the Bible. But this does not mean that the Bible is completely ignored. Luther uses the Bible as an advisory authority, containing useful models for a healthy Church life. To give two examples: he accepts the advice of St. Paul that women should not be ministers. But this is binding for him only in normal circumstances, if there are men suitable to exercise the ministry. Where there are no suitable men, e.g. in women's convents, or in emergency cases, Luther would not object to women being called to the ministry.[1]

Luther, as we saw, tries to prove from the New Testament that *one* congregation may have *several* bishops; he argues from this that one congregation may have several fully ordained ministers, and that our present condition of monarchic episcopacy cannot be deduced from the Bible. But it does not follow from this that a kind of monarchic episcopacy is unbearable for the Church. As long as it works as a good useful order for the promotion of the Gospel, it may exist in spite of its non-Biblical foundation. This is especially typical of Luther.

As for practical reforms, Luther insists that they be introduced with very great tact and without violating the most timid conscience.[2] For example: in places where he arranged for an evangelical Eucharist in which both bread and wine were taken by the communicants, he also arranged that for a transitory period, those whose conscience was troubled about the reform of the Mass, should continue the custom of taking the bread only.[3]

But it would be a misunderstanding to imagine that the ordinances and rituals of the Church could easily be disobeyed, being only man-made. For Luther, man-made orders have a very high authority and *God* demands obedience to them, as long as they are made by the proper authority and do not contradict the Word of God.

On the other hand, Luther makes it abundantly clear that

---

[1] *W.A.*, 8, 497f. (Biblical models: Joel ii. 28; Acts xxi. 8f.; 1 Cor. xi. 5f.; and Old Testament passages). *W.A.*, 10, III, 170ff.; 12, 308, 30; 389, 10.

[2] *W.A.*, 39, I, 22f.; McKinnon, *op. cit.*, III, 90–101.

[3] L. Fendt, *op. cit.*, pp. 96, 120.

liturgical forms, prayer books, ceremonial, etc., should help Christians to pray, to concentrate their minds, and to hear and learn the Word of God in a proper way. But the use of these helpful forms and ceremonies is in itself no service rendered to God, and the performance of certain rites and the saying of certain liturgies does not earn any merit before God.[1]

12. *Luther as a liturgical reformer*[2]

It is a disputed question whether Luther was very clever in organising church constitutions and in dealing with the State. It cannot, however, easily be denied that he had special musical and liturgical gifts. The hymn tunes composed by him will always hold an important place in Church music. But he had not only to compose tunes for his hymns, he was also obliged to provide liturgical melodies for the sung Eucharist in German. Some melodies could be taken over from the mediæval Church, e.g. the preface before the Sanctus, a melody which to-day Lutherans still share with Roman Catholics and Anglicans. The melodies of other parts had to be altered owing to the translation, and some quite new melodies were necessary because Luther wanted the ministers to sing some passages which were not sung even in the Roman Church. In this sphere Luther was at his best, and the melodies composed by him were simple, adapted to the meaning of the words, and completely avoided a wrong sentimentality.[3]

Luther gives no theoretical explanation of the obvious fact that in all his practical liturgical proposals he shows a definite tendency to increase the singing of the pastor at the altar beyond what was usual in the Roman Church. He even wants the pastor to sing the words of consecration in the Lord's Supper and the words of benediction at the end of the service. This attitude may have been strengthened by his opposition to Roman habits. The words of consecration which were spoken in a low voice by the Roman priest and so were unintelligible to the congregation,[4] should be loudly sung by the Lutheran minister, thus replacing one extreme by the other. Moreover, this form of service seems to have appealed to Luther's sense of beauty; it also gave the welcome opportunity to introduce responses sung by the people. Luther seems to have disliked long extempore prayers to which the congrega-

[1] *W.A.*, 19, 73; 26, 222ff.; 230ff.
[2] Cf. the report of Musculus about the Wittenberg services in 1536, in Kolde, *Analecta Lutherana*, 216ff., 226ff.; H. Preuss, *Martin Luther der Künstler*, Gütersloh, 1931.
[3] *W.A.*, 19, 44ff.; 87ff.; 97ff.; 102ff.
[4] *W.A.*, 18, 22ff.; 38, 247; *Tischr.*, 5, 589.

tion had to listen without an opportunity of responding. He also stresses the pedagogical character of the service. It ought to help people to learn Biblical texts, and to grasp the pure doctrine. Texts, however, will be learnt more easily if people are not just listening to them, but are singing them, e.g. as introits in the service, responding to the minister. So the Lutheran church became famous for its outstanding musical tradition, for its church choirs, and for its organists and composers (e.g. J. S. Bach).

For educational purposes Luther even wanted to retain some Latin Masses or even to introduce occasional Masses in Greek and Hebrew in order to make school children learn these languages which were so vital for reading the Bible in the original.[1] Actually there were some places, like Magdeburg Cathedral, where long after the Reformation the service was still occasionally sung in Latin. But, on the whole, of course, the services were to be held in the vernacular.

Luther's high estimation of liturgical singing may have been promoted by his sense of "objectivity." He does not use this word, but the matter is clearly in his mind or in his sub-consciousness. The Holy Word should not be given with the personal emphasis of the minister, because the service is not a private performance indicating the religious experience of the individual preacher. It is a service of the Church, and the liturgy, lessons and tunes appointed by the Church should be used, in the same way as the ecclesiastical year and the clerical dress fixed by the Church.

The attitude of the present-day Lutheran clergy to these liturgical questions is divided. Some like to treat the liturgical interest of Luther as his private hobby, no longer important for to-day. Some Lutheran Churches have very simple unliturgical services. Others, however, regard Luther's liturgical principles as very vital and as the proper form of expressing his religious convictions. They try to keep or reintroduce Luther's type of service at all costs. Thus, this type of fully musical Lutheran service still exists in many German dioceses, e.g. Bavaria, Hanover and Saxony, and especially in the Scandinavian Churches, and other Lutheran Churches all over the world. In the last twenty-five years, many attempts have been made to reintroduce Luther's type of service in those Churches which have lost it.

One ought never to forget that the freedom given to the Church to control liturgical matters is, in Luther's view, a freedom to alter details, but not a freedom to abolish liturgical forms altogether.[2] This has been forgotten by certain super-Protestants, who thought they had to fulfil the work started by Luther by

[1] *W.A.*, 19, 74.   [2] Cf. *W.A.*, 26, 222ff.

abolishing one liturgical form after another. To give one example: whether a minister should wear a eucharistic vestment or a surplice or a black gown only is a question open to discussion. But that he *should* wear a special dress for divine service is most desirable.[1]

In his later years Luther became more and more conservative in liturgical and ceremonial matters.[2] He tried to reintroduce rituals in Churches where they had disappeared.[3] He was afraid that the abolition of eucharistic vestments and too great deviation from Church tradition and ritual might create disorder, so that finally it would be impossible to distinguish in church the minister, peasant and caretaker.[4]

Nowadays, it has become customary to criticise Luther on two charges which in themselves cannot be reconciled with one another. He is accused by fervent Protestants, mostly Calvinists, of still being half Catholic on the matter of ritual. They think that it is scandalous that Luther went even so far as to retain the crucifix.[5] On the other hand, Catholics and Anglicans sometimes think of Luther in terms of a man who abolished all traditions, ceremonies and even creeds, and represented the first step of a development ending with the Society of Friends or the Plymouth Brethren. I myself have been asked frequently in this country whether the Lutherans had churches, altars, liturgies or ministers.

Both criticisms fail to see the real point of Luther's intentions. There is *one* impression that Luther wishes to avoid at all costs: that this reformation meant replacing one *form* by another. He is concerned with the centre of doctrine and does not want to occupy overmuch the mind of the people with the unavoidable but less important alteration of forms. If I may use a modern parable: he took the Roman Mass like a sponge which he pressed out and filled with new contents. It was no use replacing one sponge by another; it was a change of content that mattered. Luther feels that too far-reaching and unnecessary alterations of forms and ceremonies were not only useless, but even dangerous. It might be

---

[1] People must know "who is the pastor and who is farmer or citizen," *Theologische Studien und Kritiken*, 1885, 146. Köstlin-Kawerau, *op. cit.*, II, 21.

[2] *Tischr.*, 7,131; *W.A.*, 48, 693, 13.

[3] "*Dico autem potissimum de missarum ceremoniis, quales sunt altaria, vestes, candelae and huiusmodi leviculae, quae si depositae non sunt, servari possunt, sicut faciemus hic Wittembergae. Sin depositae sunt, optarim, paulatim repetere eas, regnante tamen verbo, quo conscientias liberemus.*" *Briefw.*, January 11th, 1531 (No. 1,768), cf. No. 1,822.; *W.A.*, 30, III, 1ff.; *Briefw.*, February 13th, 1529 to N. Hausmann about the reintroduction of the litany.

[4] See p. 94, note 1.

[5] Already in 1536 "Protestant" visitors in Wittenberg were astonished that the Lutheran services retained so many traditions, ceremonies and liturgical forms. Kolde, *Analecta Lutherana, ibid.*

thought that Luther did not want to reintroduce justification by faith and the authority of the Scriptures, but that he only wanted to replace the surplice by a black gown. He was amply justified by later developments.[1] In Germany, prior to Hitler, it was quite possible for a minister to preach heresies and paganism in a black preaching gown, and hardly any Church member would notice it; this at least applied to many congregations; but if the minister were to wear a Eucharistic vestment or to sing a Lutheran liturgy in those territories where it was no longer usual, everyone would be irritated by this "Roman Catholic attitude." Only after the catastrophes of 1933 did many congregations become accustomed once more to take special notice of the minister's doctrine.

It is quite wrong to think that conservatism in these questions reveals spiritual weakness or compromise. Just the contrary is true. The traditional Mass was regarded by Christians before the Reformation with a kind of religious awe, almost as inspired. We know that Luther soon after his ordination regarded the wording of the Mass with anxiety or even superstition. That he dared to alter *this* Mass, to use the holy forms and vestments for new contents, was a much more radical attack upon the mediæval Mass practice than the creation of completely new forms would have been.[2]

Luther is very hesitant to print new Lutheran liturgies, because he is afraid that the same result may happen and his followers may regard Luther's form of service as an inspired, unalterable order. For this reason he favours a certain amount of liturgical variety, as I have already said.[3]

13. *In statu confessionis nihil est adiaphoron*

Adiaphora, as we have seen, was a term describing those church constitutions and ceremonies which were neither good nor bad in themselves, but which could be used according to the best human understanding. In Church conflicts, however, it was possible that unity in these matters was used to veil differences and to arrive at some wrong sort of peace or compromise.

To give two examples: In 1547, the Emperor Charles V tried to

[1] P. Graff, *Geschichte der Auflösung der alten gottesdienstlichen Formen in der evangelischen Kirche Deutschlands*, 1921; P. Drews, *Der evangelische Geistliche in der deutschen Vergangenheit*, 1905 (16,000 copies, 1924); L. Fendt, *op. cit.*, pp. 317–19; Elert, *op. cit.*, I, 293ff.

[2] L. Fendt, *op. cit.*, p. 105.

[3] He only recommends uniformity of ritual within one city and its neighbouring villages, *W.A.*, 19, 73.

bring into operation a scheme for reunion between the Lutherans and the Roman Catholics. What he proposed was in effect that both parties should agree to adopt *one* episcopal Church constitution and one common ritual prescribing the same liturgical forms and vestments. Doctrinal matters should be left to later discussion. The Lutherans replied that doctrine was the real thing that mattered and that they felt bound to abolish traditional ceremonies (which up to now they had used with a good conscience) if these were misused in order to veil the real differences in the Church. In many Churches, vestments and certain ceremonies were actually abolished at that time.[1]

In the seventeenth and eighteenth centuries, the same thing happened the other way round. The Prussian rulers and kings, who were not Lutherans but Calvinists, tried to bring about a reunion between the Lutheran and Calvinist Churches of their country. They made decrees forbidding the ministers to preach on the doctrinal differences between the two denominations. They also tried to enforce a closer similarity between the ceremonies of Lutherans and Calvinists. The Lutherans were asked to abolish liturgical vestments, candles, the sung Mass, etc.

The Lutherans reacted in many places by reintroducing vestments and retaining them where they were still in use. In principle, it did not matter much to them whether they wore a black gown or a white surplice, but if the black gown was misused to further a wrong unity at the expense of truth, it became a matter of conscience to retain the white vestments.[2]

The principle which I have illustrated in these two examples was labelled in Reformation times by the Latin sentence: *In statu confessionis nihil est adiaphoron.* This means that there are situations in which the Church is forced to make its confession of the truth against heresies and un-Christian practices. If external Church orders or ceremonies are misused in order to prevent the Church from confessing, they are no longer *adiaphora*, but they may become of vital importance.[3]

In recent years (after 1933) this principle was frequently applied by the Confessional Church in Germany. The State tried to get complete control over the Church by interfering in matters of

[1] cf. L. Fendt, *op. cit.*, pp. 302ff. (*das Interim*); P. Drews, *Der evangelische Geistliche*, etc., pp. 37–40; E. Sehling, *Die Kirchengesetzgebung unter Moritz von Sachsen und Georg von Anhalt*, Leipzig, 1899, pp. 91–120, esp. pp. 114ff.

[2] Johannes Sonneck, *Die Beibehaltung der katholischen Formen in der Reformation Joachims II von Brandenburg und ihre allmähliche Beseitigung*; P. Drews, *Der evangelische Geistliche*, etc., p. 40; Elert, *op. cit.*, I, 294; L. Fendt, *op. cit.*, pp. 318ff.; O. Mehl, *Des Soldatenkönigs Kampf gegen die Zeremonien*, "*Hochkirche*" 1928, No. 1.

[3] *Bekenntnisschriften*, pp. 813ff., 1,053ff. (1,062, 28).

administration which in ordinary times would have been quite open to discussion. The Christians, however, knew that the seemingly unimportant laws were designed to serve as test cases and to bring the Church under complete State dictatorship. So they felt in conscience bound to resist.

V
ESCHATOLOGY[1]

IT is justifiable to write a short chapter of its own on Luther's doctrine on the Last Things. Luther has not written long treatises on this question, but modern scholars have pointed out from many occasional references in his writings that the question of eschatology was of primary importance to him. He preached that Christ, through death and Resurrection, has destroyed the power of Satan. But how could he reconcile this belief with his own conviction that the world was still full of satanic things? Christ's Easter victory was more or less a secret victory which only could be *believed*. Only the faithful knew that Christ had won the decisive battle. But the beaten enemy, sin, death and Satan, was seemingly still in power. Christ, however, would come back at the end of time and show to everybody, also to the unbelievers, that He was the real Lord and that sin, death and Satan could no longer harm us, for they were judged and had lost the battle. Still, the anti-Christ (he became more and more convinced that the Pope was the anti-Christ), the Turks, and many other evil powers exercised some sort of influence in the world. Still they could threaten the pure Gospel, persecute Luther, kill his followers, and Christ did not raise a finger to save them. No wonder that Luther could not bear life without longing for that last day[2] when Christ, as he expected, would return in glory and in His Judgment reveal what was and what was not the Truth, would publicly show that Luther's doctrine was the right one and that his opponents were wrong, would defeat the might of Pope, Turks and enthusiasts, swallow up sin, death and Devil and establish a realm of eternal life in which all resistance to God has permanently vanished.[3] This is the second Advent of Christ in which Christ openly rules over the world on the ground of that victory that He won when He came to earth the first time. This victory of Good Friday and Easter is only known to the believers, and is still concealed from the world, but will be revealed in full at this Second Advent of Christ.[4]

Luther thought that this day was near at hand. He supports

---

[1] For the whole chapter, P. Althaus, *Die letzten Dinge* (*op. cit.*); K. Heim, *Jesus der Weltvollender* (*op. cit.*); Köstlin, *op. cit.*, II, 334–50; Elert, *op. cit.*, I, 447ff.
[2] *Geb Gott, es geschehe balde, Amen. W.A.*, 8, 719, 34.
[3] *Tischr.*, 203; 491.   [4] e.g. *W.A.*, 8, 719, 29.

ESCHATOLOGY

this belief by arguments taken from the Bible and by showing that the political and ecclesiastical situation showed great similarity with the Biblical description of the time immediately preceding the Last Day.[1] When astronomers predicted a great flood for 1524, Luther hoped that this signified the Last Day. On the other hand, he does not forget to warn people to remember Christ's word that nobody knew the day and hour except God.

Is it surprising that Luther longed for the end of this world? In contrast to Catholic ascetic tendencies, he had taught his followers joyfully to accept God's good gifts in this life. But all the valuable treasures of this life were not comparable to the glorious day of the Son of Man. Modern arguments that mankind still needs much more time in order to develop culture, civilisation and democracy are totally alien to Luther's mind. He is so fully convinced of the total depravity of human nature that he does not believe in the real progress of mankind.

The glorious new world is entirely brought about by the action of Christ, not by human development. In a single moment this bad world will be transformed and a new heaven and earth appear. There will be the resurrection of all dead, and the Last Judgment. In his sermons, Luther describes this event with the expressions used in the Bible[2] (the last trumpet, Christ coming in the clouds, etc.), but he adds: "these are only allegoric words . . . as we have to picture it for children and simple folk."[3]

He believes in the eternal damnation of the godless. Their greatest pain consists in the feeling of God's wrath and the knowledge of being separated from Him.[4]

Those who are saved will live in the transformed new world in which the sun will shine seven times more brightly than now, and the moon as brightly as the sun. Now heaven and earth wear their working clothes, but then they will be in their Sunday clothes.[5] Our bodies will be as the Body of Christ after the Resurrection; no longer subject to disease and pain, to the limitations of time and place, no longer perishable and changeable. But everyone will have his own body, a spiritual body, as described in 1 Cor. xv.[6]

Luther thinks there are many certain references to this Last Day in the Bible. But he notes the fact that there are almost no references from the time between the death of the individual and

[1] Cf. J. Köstlin, *Beitrag zur Eschatologie der Reformatoren* in *Theol. Studien und Kritiken*, 1878, pp. 125ff.; see also *Tischr.*, 4,979; 5,130; 5,239; 5,488; 6,984.
[2] *Tischr.*, 1,520; *W.A.*, 10, I (2), 93–120.
[3] J. Köstlin, *Luthers Theologie* (*op. cit.*), II, 345.
[4] *Tischr.*, 6,982.
[5] Köstlin, *op. cit.*, II, 348; cf. letter to his son Hänschen, *Briefw.*, June 19, 1530.
[6] *Catechismus major. Bekenntnisschriften*, p. 659; cf. *ibid.*, p. 1,007.

the Last Day. He is strongly opposed to the idea of a purgatory which seems to suggest that there is still a possibility of development on the other side of the grave, or that salvation, given to men by the grace of God, was not sufficient and needed some kind of complement.[1] It is more tolerable in Luther's view if purgatory is explained as a place where those Christians, who have been really and completely saved by faith, are still further purged from that sin which was inherent in them up to their death. But Luther did not find any Scriptural truth for that either.[2] Luther's conception of justification by faith alone rules also his conception of the world after death. It is a problem for him whether God can save those who died without any chance of acquiring faith. Nobody can be saved without faith; but it would be a different question whether God could give faith to some during their dying or after their death and in this way save them through faith. "Who would doubt that He *could* do it? But one cannot prove that He really does it."[3] And yet Luther hopes that God will be gracious to Cicero.[4] While condemning all attempts of the living to influence the fate of the dead by Masses, good works and prayers, he yet permits a short prayer of intercession recommending them to the Grace of God.[5]

Luther likes to picture the interval between our death and the Last Judgment as a kind of sleep. Those who died in Christ will sleep in peace and comfort, and this signifies that they must have some kind of self-consciousness. They will lose all sense for a time, and when the Last Day awakens them, they may believe that they have slept only for one hour. But this sleep may be interrupted by dreams or visions sent from God, as the story of the rich man and Lazarus indicates. Again and again Luther emphasises that God's actions with regard to the dead surpass all our understanding and imagination.[6]

Luther does not believe in a future millennium; he thinks that the thousand years when Satan is to be bound were the first thousand years of the Church, when the Church was comparatively free of heresies. After these thousand years, Satan is released again and persecutes the Church by the Anti-Christ (the Pope) and the apocalyptic nations of Gog and Magog (the Turks).[7] But Luther's critical attitude to the Book of Revelation made him refrain from too fantastic speculations.

[1] *Tischr.*, 3,695.   [2] *Briefw.*, January 13th, 1529 (to Amsdorf).
[3] *W.A.*, 10, II, 325, 3; for the whole, *ibid.*, pp. 322–6.
[4] *Tischr.*, 3,925.   [5] Köstlin, *op. cit.*, II, 343.
[6] *W.A.*, 17, II, 235, 17ff.; 36, 252, 10; 37, 149–51; 43, 359ff.; 480f.
[7] *Briefw.*, March 7th, 1529 (to W. Link); October 26th, 1529 (to N. Hausmann); November 10th, 1529 (to J. Propst).

VI

LUTHER AND THE BIBLE

1. *The principle of Re-formation*

LUTHER did not want to create a new Church, but simply to re-establish the original Catholic Church which was instituted by Christ and first represented by the Apostles. His conception of the Church may be compared to an old noble Norman church building whose original style was spoilt by later alterations. Parts of the original structure were demolished, while tasteless additions altered the appearance of the building to such an extent that the intentions of the original architect were superseded. In the same way, the Church, the Foundation of Christ, had been seriously spoilt by alteration in the course of time. Important parts of its construction, e.g. the doctrine of justification by faith alone, the proclamation of the pure Gospel, the true meaning of the Lord's Supper, the right conception of the ministry, etc., fell to pieces. On the other hand, things were added which were in obvious contradiction to the original plan. It is not necessary here to enumerate again all those things which in Luther's view had spoilt the Church during the course of time. A wrong attitude to our own good works was a central error which in due course brought forth all those many greater and smaller changes which corrupted the style of the original Church. The Pope is mainly responsible, having authorised these changes.

Luther's idea of re-formation is to make the Church once more correspond to the original plan of the Founder. To find this original plan, one has to go back to the New Testament. There it is described how Christ founded His Church; what He wanted it to be; and what it looked like during its first decades, under the care of the Apostles whom Christ had chosen. To bring the Church back to this original scheme means to destroy and abolish all those innovations which spoil the old plan, and to rebuild those essential parts of the Church that had collapsed in the course of time. This Luther tried to do in the sixteenth century. But this kind of re-formation cannot be limited to the sixteenth century only. The existing Church must *always* examine her life and work, to see whether it is still in agreement with Christ's original foundation, and must constantly be prepared to strengthen or rebuild essential things which are weakened or lost, and to abolish abuses and additions which neither correspond to the original architect's draft nor to the style of the whole building: to speak plainly, the Church has to abolish all those things which can be found neither in the letter nor in the spirit of the New Testament. This is the principle of re-formation. The Church must constantly be prepared to be re-formed by its Founder. And the will of the Founder is recognised in the Bible.

Going back to the earliest Church does not, of course, mean imitating the earliest Church in a slavish way or re-introducing all its habits, forms, and constitution. We have discussed at great length the relations between the New Testament and the ceremonies and constitution of the Church. My readers will therefore not misunderstand Luther as a man who simply wants to put back the wheel of Church history for 1,500 years. But for him the *essentials*, the doctrine and principles of the Church, are still the same as 1,500 years ago. They have to be applied to each age and its problems, as Christ and the Apostles would apply them if they had lived in that age. But the spirit and problems of the various ages must not try to effect an alteration in the essential gifts invested by Christ in His Church. They are unchangeable. Luther is convinced that St. Paul and the other Apostles would completely agree with him if they had lived in the sixteenth century. For him the Apostles were Lutherans or rather (the other way round), the Lutherans were the Apostolic Church. And if it could be proved from the Scriptures that they were not, they had to reform themselves once more till they were.[1]

Returning to Christ and the earliest Church does not only mean returning to the *New* Testament, but also to the *Old*. The Old Testament was not only clearly confirmed by Christ's express words; it was clear to every reader of the New Testament that the early Church considered the Old Testament as a book which testified of Christ. The essential parts of Christian doctrine could not be understood without the Old Testament. The Gospels describe the life of Christ as the fulfilment of the Old Testament; the Apostles describe the doctrine of the Church as the only true interpretation of the Old Testament. And the great and decisive doctrine of the relation between the Law and the Gospel could not be grasped without the Old Testament. Re-formation means to Luther not only bringing the Church into harmony with the New Testament, but with the *whole* Bible.[2]

---

[1] *Wo aber Irrtum in seinen [Luther's] Schriften durch das göttliche Wort erwiesen würde, wollte er es gern widerrufen. . . . verbrennen und mit Füssen darauf treten.* W.A., 7, 867ff.

[2] Martin Luther, *Vorreden zur Heiligen Schrift*, München (Chr. Kaiser Verlag), 1934, subsequently quoted as *Vorreden*, pp. 1ff.

2. Sola Scriptura

It has been said that the two principles of Luther's Reformation were *Sola fide* and *Sola scriptura;* the first describing the central point of Luther's Reformation, the latter the way by which he arrived at this central point. The Bible as the only authority of the Church has been stressed in Luther's discussions with his opponents, in his writings and his preaching. But it is not quite easy to define exactly Luther's doctrine on the Bible.[1]

For the unprejudiced observer of our time, the situation is extremely confused by the fact that present-day Lutherans think very differently about this question, and almost all expressly claim Luther's authority for the way in which they treat the Bible. Harnack and other champions of "higher criticism" and "modernism" claim to act in Luther's spirit, drawing the "last conclusions" of his attitude to the Bible;[2] the average Continental Lutheran who represents a moderate orthodoxy accepts the main doctrines of the Bible and takes certain passages very seriously, while claiming freedom in less essential and less fundamental things, and treats part of the Bible as not only less important but perhaps even of doubtful value for the Christian. For this distinction between "fundamentals" and "non-fundamentals," between reliable and less reliable parts of the Bible, he also claims the authority of Luther.[3] But the same authority is claimed by those who believe in the inspiration of every word of the Bible.[4] Quite a number of Continental Lutherans and a very great number of American Lutherans believe that the doctrine of verbal inspiration alone represents Luther's mind correctly, while, on the other hand, even those among the Nazis who want to abolish the Old Testament and the Apostle Paul claim to act in Luther's name. And all of them bring forward quite a number of quotations from Luther which seem to support their point of view.

The Luther-interpretation of the above-mentioned Nazis is, of course, ridiculous. How absurd to imagine Luther without the Old Testament and without St. Paul! But the opinions of all the other Lutheran schools of thought mentioned above have to

[1] For the whole subject, cf. M. Reu, *Luther and the Scriptures*. The Wartburg Press, Columbus, Ohio, U.S.A., 1944, and McKinnon, *op. cit.*, IV, 283–304.

[2] A. Harnack, *Wesen des Christentums*, Leipzig, 1900, p. 174. Further literature quoted by Reu, *op. cit.*, pp. 29f.; 115; 167 (note 188) and McKinnon, *op. cit.*, IV, 299f.

[3] Cf. P. Althaus' way of using the Bible and his criticism against *Biblizismus* in *Die letzten Dinge* (*op. cit.*), pp. 62ff., 88ff., 249ff. He rejects conceptions which he admits to find even in the New Testament, *ibid.*, esp. pp. 90ff.

[4] Cf. P. E. Kretzmann, *The Foundations must Stand!*, St. Louis, Mo., U.S.A., 1936.

be taken seriously and examined carefully. The fact that Luther's attitude to the Scriptures is interpreted in so many different ways by the most learned men of his own denomination must necessarily confuse all those who wish to know what his opinion really was. If we consider the fact that Luther in all his teaching and fighting claimed to stand on the authority of the Scriptures alone as against un-Biblical traditions and philosophies, and if we remember that Luther wanted his followers to be of *one* mind on essentials of doctrine, then it is surprising that he never gives a detailed account or explanation of his attitude to the Bible. There are very many casual references, also longer passages dealing with the subject, but there are no writings in which he deals systematically and exhaustively with the doctrine of the Bible. Some scholars take this as a sign that he had a very free attitude to the Scriptures, while others interpret it as an indication that the doctrine of "verbal inspiration" was commonly held among early Lutherans, so that there was no need for Luther to deal expressly with a question on which there was no dispute. It cannot be denied that there are some quotations from Luther's writings and sayings which seem to indicate a very independent and critical judgment of the Bible—almost arbitrary, indeed. On the other hand, there are very many quotations—I should say by far the great majority—which apparently point in the opposite direction—namely, that Luther treated the whole Bible as the Word of God, as inspired, infallible, and therefore with the greatest reverence.

Faced with the divergence of most conscientious Lutheran scholars on this point, I feel it to be an extremely difficult task for me to give to the British reader a perfectly just and scholarly explanation on this point. I will try to state what seems more or less certain to me, but I will refrain from judgment on certain highly disputed points which cannot be decided without detailed investigation which would surpass the framework of this book.

Sola scriptura is certainly a principle taken very seriously by Luther. What cannot be proved from Scripture has no authority in the Church. In 1521, he made his famous declaration before the Emperor and the Diet of Worms:

> "Unless I am convinced by testimony from Scripture or evident reason [*convictus testimoniis Scripturae aut ratione evidente*]—for I believe neither the Pope nor the Councils alone, since it is established that they have often erred and contradicted themselves—I am conquered by the writings [i.e. quotations from the Bible] cited by me, and my conscience is captive to the Word of God; recant I will and can nothing,

since it is neither safe nor honest to do aught against conscience."[1]

These famous words are often misinterpreted as if Luther put evident reason and the individual conscience as an authority besides or even above the Bible. As for the conscience, however, it ought to be clear that Luther speaks of a conscience which is completely ruled (captive) by the Word of God. As for the expression *ratio evidens*, we have to admit that it *seems* to be ambiguous and, as I said previously (p. 21), his attitude to reason seems to be ambiguous in many of his writings, as he praises and insults reason alternately. But the situation is not so obscure for those who examine Luther's utterances on reason more carefully and who try to find out how Luther actually used reason in his own thought and teaching. Luther condemns that reason which tries to be wiser than the Word of God, or, at least, as wise as the Word of God, the reason that wants to be an authority criticising the Word of God, or inventing laws and doctrines *in addition* to the Word of God.[2] This reason is the sign of human pride in unregenerate souls.

It is totally different with the humble reason of regenerate man. This reason accepts the truths revealed in the Word of God and draws conclusions by combining the various parts of this revelation. This reason tries to serve the Word of God, not to rule over it. Luther has no objection to what we call the "ministerial" use of reason in believing Christians; he condemns, however, the "magisterial" use of reason.[3] Also, reason has to be "captive to the Word of God," not its master. Moreover, human reason has its importance for those *adiaphora*, external ceremonies which are neither demanded nor forbidden by the Word of God—as we have previously seen.

If there are statements in the Bible which seem to contradict one another according to human reason and logic, the Bible is right and human reason and logic have to give way. For, after the lapse of Adam, human reason is obscured to such an extent that it cannot itself see the truth. The Bible, however, can. Zwingli and other opponents challenged Luther that his doctrine on the Lord's Supper was unreasonable and illogical. They said

---

[1] Translation quoted from Reu, *op. cit.*, p. 28; for the use of "reason" in Luther, *ibid.*, pp. 28-37. About the Latin text, cf. K. Aner, *Kirchengeschichte, III* (*op. cit.*), p. 51.

[2] *Denn er will und kann's nicht leiden, dass die Seinen etwas vornehmen zu tun, das er nicht befohlen hat, es sei wie gut es immer sein kann;* Vorreden, p. 5; Cf. *W.A.,* 6, 204; 8, 141; 142; 143; 145; *Tischr.*, 5,601.

[3] *Tischr.*, 439; *W.A.*, 9, 35; 46; 62; 40, II, 593, 24ff.; 50, 282ff.; *Briefw.*, Vol. 2, 125, 11ff. (June, 1520), No. 301.

that Christ could not have given His body to His disciples to eat in the same night in which He was betrayed because He was still in the flesh, and that the Body of Christ after His Resurrection and Ascension could not be at the same time in Heaven and in thousands of churches where the Lord's Supper was celebrated. God, they added, would not demand that we accept incompatible things. Luther answered that God certainly demands that we accept things which seem to be incompatible to our reason, e.g. that Christ was true man and God at the same time, that He was born of a virgin, etc.[1]

When the authority of the Bible was threatened in the German Churches in 1934, a great number of German Lutherans and Calvinists sent delegates to a Synod at Barmen, where they summarised their opinion in this way:

"Jesus Christ, as He is testified to us in Holy Scripture, is the one Word of God which we have to hear and which we have to trust and obey in life and death.

"We reject the false doctrine that the Church can and must acknowledge, as a source of its proclamation, beside and in addition to this one Word of God, other events, powers, forms and truths as the revelation of God."[2]

Those Lutherans who signed this declaration certainly believed that they acted in agreement with Luther's principle, *sola scriptura*.

Luther allows reason to serve as the handmaiden of theology in order to find out, as far as possible, the original wording of Biblical texts. He knows that the Hebrew and Greek editions of the Bible of his time were not free from mistakes. Textual criticism is allowed, provided that its only aim is to arrive at the original version written down by the authors. Luther likes to remedy seeming contradictions between different versions of the same event by indicating the errors of copyists.[3] Divergences in figures given in the Books of Kings and Chronicles are harmonised in this way.[4] Human reason can be used for rectifying human errors. But it is not allowed to criticise the contents of the original texts.[5]

---

[1] *Quod multa proponat nobis deus incomprehensibilia.* W.A., 30, III, 120, 17; cf. Tischr., 4,915, 5,015; cf. W.A., 15, 394, 12ff.; cf. Reu, *op. cit.*, 49ff.

[2] Cf. "The Significance of the Barmen Declaration for the Œcumenical Church," *Theology*, Occasional Papers, New Series, No. 5, London (S.P.C.K.), 1943.

[3] Reu, *op. cit.*, 105ff.

[4] W.A., *Deutsche Bibel*, 3, 419, 8ff.

[5] For quotations cf. Reu, *op. cit.*, pp. 103-8.

3. The canon of the Bible

We have seen that Luther tried to claim the authority of the Bible as against the tradition of the Church. It was not astonishing that his opponents replied by arguing that it was the tradition of the Church which was responsible for the selection of those special books that now form the canon of the Bible. Why did Luther recognise tradition on this one point while denying it in many other respects?[1]

Luther replied by using three lines of argument. (*a*) He appealed from the corrupted Church of his time to the authority of the relatively uncorrupted early Church; (*b*) he stressed the "inner" argument by pointing out the harmony and agreement connecting the various Biblical books; (*c*) and finally, he referred to the reliability of the authors. Luther does not feel it to be incongruous to use all three arguments.

(1) Luther does not actually claim that the early Church was perfect, but nevertheless it was the golden age of the Church. He is anxious to demonstrate that *he* and not the Pope is in agreement with the Fathers of the first Christian centuries. The witness of the Early Church gives an undisputed authority to those books of our present Bible which were called *Homologoumena*. This expression covers those books which by unanimous agreement were considered by the Early Church to be part of the Biblical canon. On the other hand, there were disputed books which were not accepted as canonical in wide circles of the Early Church: these disputed books are called *Amphiballomena*, or, when they are rejected more strongly, *Antilegomena*.[2] Luther thinks that some of them really must be considered of doubtful value. Four of them—namely, Hebrews, James, Judas and the Revelation—contain, on the one hand, a good amount of sound Apostolic doctrine, but, on the other hand, great errors, and their emphasis is often misleading.[3] They can certainly not claim full authority in the Church. The best of these books is Hebrews. It cannot have been written by an Apostle, but only by a pupil of an Apostle. It is a very fine book and sound in most parts, but not in all. The conception that a Christian who, after his repentance and conversion, again fell into great sin had no second chance of salvation (Chapters vi and x) was a hard blow against the unanimous witness of the undisputed New Testament books.[4] In later years, Luther finds a different interpretation more acceptable to him.[5] His

---

[1] For the whole, cf. W. Elert, *op. cit.*, I, 168–76.
[2] Cf. A. Jülicher, *Einleitung in das Neue Testament*, ed., Tübingen, 1931, pp. 515ff.
[3] *Vorreden*, p. 105, note 1; Reu, *op. cit.*, pp. 11, 44f.
[4] *Vorreden*, pp. 105f.; *Tischr.*, 5,973.
[5] Köstlin, *op. cit.*, II, 32.

judgment on Revelation was never quite clear. He expresses strong criticism about the dark meaning of many passages, and thinks that the emphasis is not on the most important part of the Gospel. But he does not take all authority from this book,[1] and says many good things about it. St. James's Epistle, however, is a really dangerous and bad book. It militates against the central idea of justification by faith. Later Lutherans tried (and are still trying) to interpret this letter in harmony with St. Paul's understanding of the Gospel; in their view, this Epistle only fights against a lawless Christianity and an antinomian misunderstanding of the doctrine of justification. Luther, however, thinks it cannot be harmonised with St. Paul's teaching.[2] The Epistle cannot have been written by an Apostle, but may have been written by a Jew who has heard the bells ringing about the Christians, but does not know where they hang.[3] He is most consistent in this criticism during his whole life. Towards the end of his life, he still makes remarks such as: "Here at Wittenberg we nearly thrust James out of the Bible";[4] "Some day I will use James to heat my stove."[5]

In his New Testament translation of 1522 Luther alters the order of the Books by putting Hebrews, James, Judas and Revelation last, indicating that these four, strictly-speaking, do not belong to the Bible.[6] For him also the Old Testament Apocrypha do not belong to the Bible (in contrast to the Roman Catholic practice). But in the same way in which Luther does not exclude the four disputed New Testament Books from his printed Bible edition, he does not even exclude the Old Testament Apocrypha. They are, however, clearly distinguishable from the canonical Old Testament text, and Luther's preface indicates that they have not the same value as the Bible, but nevertheless are good and useful reading.[7] In 1825 the British and Foreign Bible Society protested against this Lutheran use of printing the Old Testament Apocrypha with the Bible, as mixing together the Word of God with the word of man.

(2) In the previous paragraphs we have seen how vital in Luther's eyes was the witness of the Early Church when he wanted

---

[1] *Vorreden*, pp. 110ff.

[2] Nevertheless there are some valuable thoughts in it; the author had good intentions, but was not equal to his task. *Vorreden*, pp. 107ff.; Reu, *op. cit.*, pp. 38–48.

[3] *welcher wohl hat hören von den Christen läuten, aber nicht gar zusammen schlagen. . . Das haben auch die Alten gesehen, darum haben sie die epistolam nicht pro catholica epistola gehalten. Tischr.*, 5,443.

[4] *Tischr.*, 5,974.

[5] *Ich werde einmal mit dem Jeckel den Ofen heizen. Tischr.*, 5,854.

[6] See above, p. 111, note 3.

[7] Can be found in any Luther Bible containing the **Apocrypha**.

to decide which books were clearly canonical and which were disputed. But we saw that he did not accept the witness of the Early Church blindly; he took the contents of the books in order to justify the decision of the Early Church. In his eyes the Early Church only acted as a kind of tribunal bearing testimony as to which of the books contained the true Gospel. The authority of the Biblical books is, therefore, not only derived from the authority of the Early Church, but from the authority of the Christian content of the books. This "inner" authority still carries weight at the present time as it did in the early days of the Church. This "inner" argument is therefore to be used besides and in addition to the "historic" argument.

The undisputed canonical books do not contradict each other, but, although differing in outlook and emphasis, they fit into one and the same divine revelation. They all testify both to the Law and the Gospel. There are books which preach mainly the Law, and others which preach mainly the Gospel, but there are passages relating to the Gospel within the former, and passages relating to the Law within the latter.[1] All the books of the canon essentially refer to Christ and proclaim Him, even if they do not mention His name. The only proper starting-point for the right interpretation of the canonical books is the revelation of God in Jesus Christ, who fulfils the Law and through whom the Gospel is offered to the world. Here lies the essential connection between the canonical books.

Luther is often quoted as saying: the Bible is the Word of God in so far as it is concerned with Christ[2] (*soweit sie Christum treibet*). Luther, it is true, often spoke in this way.[3] But I am certain that we misunderstand him if we infer that Luther means us to *select* certain parts of the Bible as especially "Christian" and reject other parts as non-Christian. He believes that in the deepest sense all parts of the canonical books refer to Christ. It is the modern outlook to look upon parts of the Old Testament as irrelevant to Christianity, e.g. the story of Creation and the patriarchs, the Laws and dealings of Moses with the people, the story of the prophet Jonah, etc. It must, however, have been clear to Luther as a diligent Bible-reader that Christ and the Apostles refer to these parts of the Old Testament as having an

---

[1] *Vorreden*, p. 2; cf. M. Reu, *Luther's German Bible*, Columbus, Ohio, 1934, pp. 101–14.

[2] "*Darin stimmen alle rechtschaffenen heiligen Bücher überein, dass sie allesamt Christum predigen und treiben, auch ist das der rechte Prüfestein, alle Bücher zu tadeln, wenn man siehet, ob sie Christum treiben oder nicht.*" *Vorreden*, p. 107; cf. *W.A.*, 40, III, 652, 12ff.

[3] e.g. *Christum und das Evangelion zu suchen im Alten Testament. Vorreden*, p. 14.

H

important bearing on God's revelation in Christ. Luther calls the Book of Genesis "almost an evangelical book."[1] He finds in it the doctrine of the Trinity, the doctrine of the first and second Adam, and justification by faith (in Abraham), and this interpretation of the Book of Genesis is expressly confirmed by St. Paul.[2] Even the Old Testament worship with its many kinds of sacrifices was a foreshadowing of the sacrifice of our Easter Lamb, Christ, and Old Testament priesthood and worship came to an end because it was fulfilled in Christ.[3] This way of interpreting the Old Testament is contained in those parts of Hebrews which are highly esteemed by Luther, and in practically the whole of the New Testament. It is true that Luther also has a high esteem for those parts of the Old Testament which Christian modernists prefer and value: the Psalms, the Prophets, etc. But he esteems these books, not so much for their high morals, their beautiful poetry and their "almost Christian" ethical approach to religion, as for the Law and Gospel contained in them.[4] Also, these books proclaim the revelation of God in Christ and the justification by Faith alone. We have to remember that Luther detected this central doctrine of Justification by Faith, not during his New Testament studies, but while he was preparing his lecture on the Psalms.[5]

Some people who have heard about Luther's criticism of the Epistle of St. James because in his view it did not proclaim the Gospel of Christ, may think that Luther applied a principle of *selection* all through the Bible and excluded those passages "which were not concerned with Christ." But he did not apply this principle of selection to *canonical* books, and we must be careful to bear this distinction in mind: St. James, like Hebrews, Judas and the Revelation, were not canonical books to him, because he could not manage to reconcile *all* the passages of these books with the central Christian Gospel message. He could do this, however, with the canonical books. The principle "as far as it concerns Christ" is a principle of *interpretation*, not of *selection*.

But Luther has to admit that some of the canonical books refer to the central Gospel message in a much clearer and stronger sense than others. From this point of view, there are some books

---

[1] *Vorreden*, p. 3; *Tischr.*, 4,964.

[2] *ibid.*; cf. Luther's lectures on Genesis. W.A., 42–W.A., 44.

[3] Cf. *Vorreden*, pp. 3–15.

[4] Examples: Isaiah (*Vorreden*, p. 41), Jeremiah (*ibid.*, p. 45), Daniel (*ibid.*, p. 55); cf. W.A., 20, 576–80 (Jeremiah).

[5] W.A., 51, 1–11; *Vorreden*, pp. 18–25; "*Und sollt der Psalter allein deshalben teuer und lieb sein, dass er von Christus Sterben und Auferstehen so klärlich verheisset und sein Reich und der ganzen Christenheit Stand und Wesen vorbildet. Dass es wohl möcht eine kleine Biblia heissen, darin alles aufs schönste und kürzeste so in der ganzen Biblia steht, gefasset....*" *Vorreden*, p. 19.

in the Bible which can be called the most important or main books, while others are less important. But this does not mean that these other books are wrong and valueless.[1] Among those books which are of especially high value are not only Genesis, the Letters of St. Paul or the First Letter of St. Peter, but also the Gospel of St. John which, in Luther's view, is the "main Gospel," of more value than the Synoptic Gospels.[2] This does not, of course, mean that Matthew, Mark and Luke are without value. But St. John's Gospel is more important.

(3) The third line in Luther's argument, as to why certain books were included in the canon of the Bible and others were rejected, refers to the fact that they were written by specially reliable authors. In connection with this there are two points worth mentioning: firstly, they were reliable for more or less *historic* reasons, i.e. their authors were eye-witnesses of important happenings, in Old or New Testament time; some of them witnessed the life, death and Resurrection of Christ or had been taught and sent by Christ; they were Apostles and disciples of Apostles.

Secondly, the writers of Holy Scriptures were in a special way *inspired* by the Holy Ghost. This refers also to the Prophets and great writers of the Old Testament. We must deal with this point later.

We have seen that Luther recognises the authority of the canon for three reasons: (1) the authority of the Early Church, (2) the harmony and agreement connecting the various Biblical books and (3) the reliability of the authors. The first two arguments are connected and are based mainly not on philological or historical but on *theological* considerations. Modern "higher criticism" cannot influence these arguments much. Only the third argument can come into conflict with "higher criticism": if it can be proved that certain books are not written by reliable authors, Apostles and their disciples, etc., but by authors whose information was not first-hand, the authority of these books would necessarily decrease in value. For this reason, those Lutherans who stressed this third line of argument were very reluctant to accept the results of "higher criticism." In present-day Continental Lutheranism, there is something like a counter-movement: "higher criticism" is in its turn criticised (by some, not by all!) as being most unreal, unreliable and liable to miss the point. Many American Lutherans have always taken this line.

---

[1] Reu, *op. cit.*, p. 72. Even Ecclesiastes is valuable as a book against Free Will. *Vorreden*, pp. 29f.

[2] *Vorreden*, pp. 74f.; Romans as the key to the interpretation of the whole Bible, *Vorreden*, pp. 71f., 78ff.; cf. *Tischr.*, 5,585.

4. The Bible as "the Word of God"

The greatest argument in favour of the authority of the Bible is the fact that the preaching of Biblical truth creates faith in men's hearts. Sinful and fallen man, the enemy of God, recognises sin and is saved by faith, his mind is set at rest, and he becomes once more God's dear child. This is the stupendous miracle which proves the authority of the Bible. For Luther, this miracle is a much stronger argument than all historical considerations and weaker arguments and miracles.[1] This is the "testimony of the Holy Spirit" witnessing to the authority of the Bible by using Biblical preaching to create faith.

This "Biblical preaching" is based on the Bible, as the phrase implies. But it is not quite the same as the printed or written Bible. The Apostles preached this "Biblical message" before it became "Biblical," i.e. before it was written down; and the written or printed Bible cannot create faith *extra usum*, i.e. if it is not used, preached or read.[2] Luther calls the "Biblical message," i.e. the preaching of the truth contained in the Bible, "the Word of God." He also calls the printed or written Bible, "the Word of God," it is the Word of God "put into letters" (*gebuchstabet*).[3] It is the preached Word of God written down, and new preaching of the Word of God arises when the contents of this book are preached. The proclaimed "Word of God" is therefore derived from the written "Word of God" and *vice versa*. And Jesus Christ is the "Word of God" to us in a special sense; He is the key to the interpretation of the Bible.[4]

The decisive proof of the authority of the "Word of God" is, as we have seen, the testimony of the Holy Spirit, i.e. the fact that the Holy Spirit at all times and still to-day thereby creates faith. But what is the reason that the authors of the Biblical books, in their time, were able to write down texts that can be called "the Word of God put into letters" and with what texts is this special authority connected? Were the authors "inspired" in a special manner? It cannot be denied that Luther believes that the Holy Ghost has moved the Biblical writers. There are many quotations which say that the Holy Ghost speaks in the words of the Bible, as if He were the real author of the Bible or, at least, as if He moved

---

[1] Cf. K. v. Hase, *Hutterus Redivivus* (*op. cit.*), p. 75, § 37; *W.A.*, 3, 300; 587.

[2] Cf. *W.A.*, 21, 466, 36.

[3] "*Die heilige Schrift ist Gottes Wort, geschrieben und (dass ich so rede) gebuchstabet und in Buchstaben gebildet, gleich wie Christus ist das ewige Wort Gottes, in die Menschheit verhüllet.*" *W.A.*, 48, 31, 4, i.e. the Bible has a divine and a human nature in the same way as Christ; we could say: it is a true book and the true Word of God.

[4] *W.A.*, 17, II, 310–27.

the authors to write down the truth revealed by the Holy Ghost.[1] There are sentences in which Luther claims that Moses' and St. Paul's Biblical writings must fit together, as the Holy Ghost cannot be against Himself. The question whether Moses himself has written all five books ascribed to him by tradition, i.e. the question of the historical authorship of the Biblical books, has not much relevancy for Luther.[2] But it *is* relevant that these books —whoever has written them—were inspired by the Holy Spirit.

Protestant theology after Luther developed the doctrine of "verbal inspiration" of all the canonical books of the Bible. This does not necessarily imply a mechanical theory of dictation; the differences in the gifts of the individual authors can be used by the Holy Spirit for His purpose.[3] But it would mean that the authors were inspired to write down these very facts and thoughts. In this case each sentence, thought, and even word of the original texts has its meaning and was inspired by the Holy Ghost, and our own reason is not allowed to make critical distinctions between "reliable" and "unreliable" Bible words. The only task left for our reason is to try hard to reconstruct the original text as far as possible.

Luther himself does not formulate this doctrine in specific terms. But as we saw, many theologians think that this doctrine would be the right expression of his conviction, and that he used the Bible in a way which made it clear that for him everything in it was inspired. Others, however, take the opposite point of view, claiming that every such doctrine is in complete contradiction to his manner of using the Scriptures.[4] It is this doctrine which has more than once divided Lutherans from one another.

Those who claim that Luther treated the Scriptures in an absolutely "free" manner, and that he was opposed to any idea of "verbal inspiration," very often refer to his well-known criticism of Hebrews, St. James, etc. This argument, as we have seen, is not conclusive, as these books, for Luther, are not part of the canon. On the contrary: the fact that Hebrews contained one or two conceptions which Luther could not agree with makes him doubt

---

[1] Examples: *W.A.*, 48, 31, 24; 48, 43; cf. Reu, *op. cit.*, pp. 18; 56f.; 62f.; 109ff. A good collection of quotations in *Lehre und Wehre, herausgegeben von der deutschen ev. Luth. Synode von Missouri, Ohio u.a. Staaten*, 49. *Jahrgang*, pp. 275ff., 296ff., 336ff., 50. *Jahrgang*, pp. 164ff. (St. Louis, Mo., 1903 and 1904).

[2] Tischr., 291, 4,964. "*Deinde Magister Forstemius dixit multos asserere pentateuchon a Mose non fuisse scriptum. Respondet Dominus Doctor (Luther): Quid hoc ad rem? Esto Moses non scripserit, attamen est Mosi liber. . . .*" Tischr., 2,844b.

[3] cf. Reu, *op. cit.*, pp. 109-32.

[4] e.g. F. Hildebrandt, *Est, Das Lutherische Prinzip* (*op. cit.*), pp. 86ff.

the authority of this book.¹ This applies even more to St. James and Revelation. He does not say: "these books contain a few conceptions contrary to St. Paul, but that does not matter. Not every word of the Bible is absolutely binding." On the contrary: the fact that there were words in Hebrews, James, etc., which were not absolutely binding, makes him conclude that these books are not parts of the Bible. I have not found any quotation of Luther's indicating that a passage in one of the undisputedly canonical books contains the wrong thoughts. It is true that not every word spoken by God and written down in the Bible remains valid for us to-day, e.g. God's commandment to Noah to go into the Ark, or certain ceremonial laws. But nevertheless they *were* God's Word and they were written by inspiration of the Holy Spirit, and they have still some meaning for us (as examples, as part of "the Law," etc.)² It is true there are *dark* words in the Bible that must be explained with the help of the *clear* words of the Bible.³ There are even words which Luther confesses not to understand. In this case, he says, he will take off his hat in order to pay reverence to this word, and go on to the next passage.⁴ All this is true, but I think it is obvious that Luther takes every word of the Bible very seriously and never tries to get rid of difficulties by claiming simply that *not all* passages of the Bible were inspired and reliable. There are more or less important, more or less "evangelical," more or less clear words or passages in the Bible; there may be doubt as to how to interpret a difficult passage.⁵ But its authority is never doubted; for it is written in the Bible. In this sense "it is written" means "God has spoken," and "it is written" is the main argument in Luther's theological disputes.

But has any passage in the Bible an authority dissociated from the main theme of the Word of God, the theme of the Law and the Gospel, or the revelation of God in Christ? Must not all passages be related to this central point? This raises the question: what about those occasional remarks which apparently have no importance for this central theme of the Word of God, for instance, remarks pertaining to the sphere of historical facts and natural science? Must the Christian accept every happening recorded in the Bible as historical; must he believe in the astronomical and scientific conceptions of the Bible?

---

[1] Hebrews contains gold, silver and precious stones mixed with wood, straw and hay. *Vorreden*, p. 106. This does not apply to canonical books; cf. Reu, *op. cit.*, pp. 68–71.

[2] The importance of Moses for his time as distinct from his authority for later generations and for the Christians. *Vorreden*, pp. 6ff.

[3] e.g. Amos 1; see *Vorreden*, p. 59.   [4] *W.A.*, 20, 571, 23.

[5] In such cases he may say: *Doch halte ein jeglicher was er will*; e.g. about Obadiah 20, see *Vorreden*, p. 61.

I believe I am not wrong in admitting that Luther's utterances on these points are ambiguous. On the whole, he recognises the trustworthiness of historical records in the Bible.[1] But there are, on the other hand, words like these:

"For all the prophets of the Old Testament have chiefly deserved the name because they prophesied concerning Christ (as Peter says, Acts iv and Peter i). Furthermore, because they guided the people *in their day* by the right explanation and understanding of God's Word, rather than because they occasionally proclaimed something concerning kings and worldly princes, which they did only seldom and *in which they often erred*. But the other form of prophecy they exercised daily and were not deceived. For faith does not err in those whose prophecy is like theirs. (*Italics mine.*)[2]

"The writer of Chronicles noted only the summary and chief stories and events. Whatever is less important and immaterial he passed by. For this reason, the Books of the Kings are more credible than the Chronicles."[3]

And yet he tries to remove contradictions between Kings and Chronicles, or between St. John and the synoptics. And these and similar quotations are really not quite lucid, and different interpretations are possible.[4]

As regards natural science, Luther is still more ambiguous. In very many cases it appears that he treats the story of Creation and other Biblical statements belonging to the sphere of science—biology, geography—as literal expressions of facts.[5] On the other hand, he is convinced that these scientific descriptions do not always explain things as they *are*, but as they *appear* to the spectator.[6] Elert and other scholars tried to prove, with forceful

[1] e.g. the Biblical chronology of the prophets, *Vorreden*, pp. 55ff.

[2] *W.A.*, 17, II, 39, 27. It is, however, doubtful whether this passage refers to canonical writings, cf. Reu, *op. cit.*, pp. 65ff.

[3] *Tischr.* 1, 364; Reu. *op. cit.*, p. 72; this may, however, only mean that Kings are more detailed; cf. Luther's attempts of harmonizing seeming contradictions; if we read in Chronicles that many people are killed in battle, e.g. 80,000, and Kings give a smaller number, Luther thinks that only 1,000 may have been killed and that the number 80,000 may refer to the whole nation which was conquered through the defeat of its army and the death of 1,000 soldiers. "*Sonst kann ich's nicht conciliieren,*" *Tischr.*, 5,560.

[4] About Luther's attempts at harmonising seeming contradictions in Scripture, cf. Reu, *op. cit.*, pp. 77–102; "according to Luther, the evangelists did not purpose to recount everything in chronological order, neither did they do so in fact. They only did so when, as in the case of Luke, they pledged themselves to observe a strict sequence." Reu, *ibid.*, p. 88; cf. *W.A.*, 26, 460, 16ff.

[5] *Tischr.*, 3,862, 5,505; cf. Reu, *op. cit.*, pp. 91–102.

[6] *W.A.*, 31, I, 370, 15; *Tischr.*, 5,259.

arguments and quotations, that questions of science for Luther belonged to the sphere of "the world" and therefore have to be explored by natural means; God's revelation in the Bible is concerned with different things and therefore cannot interfere with the freedom of science, while, on the other hand, the results of science cannot endanger the Christian faith.[1] These arguments are very impressive, and certainly indicate correctly one attitude in Luther. But there is, I think, a certain ambiguity. Luther rejects the ideas of Copernicus because his system contradicts the Bible,[2] But he seems not to mind one of Copernicus' pupils proclaiming his master's ideas in Wittenberg University. Luther does not try to influence the University authorities in order to prevent his making a journey to Copernicus; the University keeps his lectureship open while he is away.[3] The Lutherans allowed the books of Copernicus to be published in Lutheran countries and his system to be taught in the universities. It is certain that Luther would have criticised this practice if he had felt greatly disturbed. We have seen (pp. 45f.), that for him Heaven is not a fixed place overhead, but is everywhere, because Christ "sitteth on the right hand of God the Father" and "on the right hand of God" means everywhere. This opinion, which he formed in connection with the doctrine on the Lord's Supper, allows him to refrain from fighting Copernicus, as the latter's system does not clash with Luther's theology. The Biblical predictions on the end of the World are sometimes described by Luther as "allegoric words . . . as we have to picture it for children and simple folk," not as scientific descriptions of geological and astronomic happenings. But, as we have seen, there are other passages where he seems to take these predictions literally and uses both Bible and astronomy in order to support his conviction concerning the Last Day (see above, pp. 102 ff.).

5. *Luther's interpretation of the Bible*

Luther tries to give a most comprehensive interpretation of the *whole* Bible. *All* parts of the Bible, even those which seem more remote to the Christian, must find their place in the framework of his interpretation. To achieve this, Scripture must be interpreted by Scripture. For example: all laws claiming to have been given to the people of Israel by God were in fact so given by God. He would not accept "modern" ideas, current in his day and ours, that these laws were unworthy of the Christian God, and were in

---
[1] W. Elert, *op. cit.*, I, 363ff.; W. Künneth, *Evangelische Wahrheit!*, Berlin, 1937, pp. 20f.
[2] *Tischr.*, 855, 4,638.
[3] Elert, *op. cit.*, I, 369ff.

fact given by well meaning men claiming God's authority, and reflecting Jewish conceptions of God. No; all these laws were indeed given by God, but the New Testament proclaims a new covenant by which God Himself has altered His previous command. The New Testament describes which of the laws are definitely abolished for Christians, which laws still stand, how God's law must be understood and interpreted for the Christian, and what the Law meant in the framework of God's dealings with men.[1] By finding the right relation between the Law and the Gospel Luther finds the interpretation in the framework of which seemingly contradictory Biblical passages find their proper place. So he arrived at an interpretation covering the whole of the Bible. Scripture can only be interpreted by Scripture, and Scripture cannot be broken (John x. 35) except through the Will of God revealed in Scripture.[2]

For Luther, every Christian has a right and duty to read the Bible and to judge for himself its meaning and interpretation. This right is not reserved for priests, professors, bishops or the Pope.[3] But—and this is most astonishing—he is perfectly convinced that no reasonable Christian of goodwill could arrive at an interpretation of the Bible different from his own.[4] Many of his opponents quoted Biblical passages against Luther and claimed that their interpretation of the Bible compelled them to fight against him. Luther, however, is convinced that these opponents either were people of obscure judgment who lacked adequate learning, or that they were people of ill-will who based their interpretation on selected parts of the Bible apart from their context, misinterpreted in a one-sided manner, while they ignored other important parts of the Bible.[5] Everyone who honestly and diligently tried to understand the Bible *as a whole* would certainly in the end arrive at Luther's interpretation.

Luther is, therefore, convinced that *his* is *the* only possible interpretation of the Bible, and that *his* is the only pure doctrine *of the Church*.[6] We find quotations such as the following:

[1] *Vorreden*, pp. 6ff.; pp. 78ff.

[2] *Vorreden*, pp. 70ff.; even the Old Testament indicates that a new covenant will replace the old covenant; W.A., 20, 576, 14; cf. A. R. Vidler, *Christ's Strange Work* (op. cit.).

[3] W.A., 6, 411ff.; 11, 409ff.; 14, 32ff.; 21, 421, 11; 53, 233ff., esp. 242f.; see above, p. 76, note 4.

[4] W.A., 36, 491, 22ff.

[5] *Qui ex parte pugnant contra scripturam*, W.A., 39, II, 58ff.

[6] W.A., 8, 685; 10, II, 107, 11; 10, III, 258ff.; 15, 266, 14; 38, 127; *Tischr.*, 130; 6,847; Early Church and Church Fathers agree with Luther: W.A., 38, 294ff.; 51, 487ff.; *Tischr.*, 347; 4,321.

Christ "who is the Master of my doctrine and also will witness on the Last Day that this doctrine is not mine but His own pure Gospel."[1]

"Thus I say also: 'the Gospel is mine,' in order to distinguish it from other preachers' doctrine who have not got my doctrine. Therefore I say: 'it is mine, Luther's doctrine.' But I also add: 'it is not my doctrine, for, dear Lord, I have not invented it in my own head, it has not grown or sprung up in my garden, nor is it born of me, but it is God's gift and not a fiction of men.' And thus both things are true: it is mine, also it is not mine."[2]

As I have said previously, Luther does not like to speak of a "Lutheran Church": for him, the Lutherans are the true Church and all other denominations have more or less deviated from the true Church which existed from the very beginning of Christianity.[3]

"Behold, this is called the right Catholic Universal Christian Church, which will certainly not excommunicate or persecute us but be willing from its heart to accept our doctrine and confirm it and to regard us as its dear brethren. If the Pope, not respecting this real Church, excommunicates us and condemns us to hell, we can gladly bear it and despise it. But we wait for the Judge from heaven, our Lord and Saviour, who will distinguish (between the two Churches) and will decide in our favour and give to us the name of the true Church—which they, the Pope's Church, now take from us—and will publicly show the Pope's Church to be the bride of the devil."[4]

Sometimes Luther seems troubled with doubts as to whether he really can be as sure as that.[5] But he finds comfort in the thought that these doubts, as well as the opposition of his enemies, are devices of the devil, who is furious that the true saving Gospel should once again be revealed and proclaimed.[6] On the whole it is safe to say that Luther is fully convinced that his doctrine is free from errors and mistakes.[7] While he emphasises that all human work is full of sin, he does not apply this principle to his teaching and preaching. If he has preached a sermon and proclaimed his

---

[1] *W.A.*, 10, II, 106, 2.
[2] *W.A.*, 33, 354, 12.
[3] *W.A.*, 15, 266, 14; 38, 127; 38, 294ff.; 50, 514; 51, 487ff.; *Tischr.*, 347; 4,321; 6,847.
[4] *W.A.*, 46, 11, 22.
[5] *Tischr.*, 130.
[6] *W.A.*, 32, 151, 27; H. Grisar, *Luther*, Freiburg, 1911-12, I, 463; 466ff.; II, 95f.; III, 301-17.
[7] *W.A.*, 7, 294; his way of speaking in *W.A.*, 8, 685; 691ff.; *W.A.*, 17, II, 437f.; 38, 237, 7; 51, 515; *Tischr.*, 4,637.

doctrine, he is convinced that he has no need to pray for the remission of sins, because here for once he has done something which is entirely good.[1]

This does not mean that Luther claims infallibility for every sentence which he has ever spoken or written. It is obvious that a man whose words and writings fill many volumes, and whose activities extend over some decades, shows some development and many contradictions on minor points. But once he has discovered the fundamental truths of his doctrine he remains very consistent on all essential points (see above, p. 31ff.).

While Luther does not allow any compromise where the essentials of his doctrine are at stake, he is inclined to treat leniently some followers who, while accepting the essentials of his doctrine, deviate from him on minor points. This fact is stressed by members of some Lutheran Churches who claim to act in Luther's spirit when entering into close co-operation or even reunion with other Protestant Churches whose doctrine differs from Luther's doctrine on various and, as they think, less essential, points. For this reason it is highly interesting to find out where Luther was prepared to compromise and where he was not.

It is quite clear that Luther considered compromise only on points which either were not decided by the Bible or where the interpretation of Biblical texts was not quite clear.[2] Moreover—in spite of the above-mentioned condemnation of the Pope's Church!—it is on the whole safe to say that he is more inclined to compromise with certain Roman Catholic doctrines than with Puritans, Anabaptists and super-Protestants. He is quite prepared to discuss certain theological subjects with the Catholics. Sometimes he is even inclined to compromise with people who believe in the "transubstantiation" as long as they do not force their opinion on others, while, on the other hand, he is quite unable to reach any compromise with those who do not believe in the "real presence" of Christ's Body and Blood in the Lord's Supper.[3] People who deny the validity of infant baptism,[4] or believe that God demands the destruction of pictures, images and ornaments in churches, are more dangerous than the Pope and no compromise whatever can be hoped for.[5] This also applies to all sorts of

[1] *Tischr.*, 316; *W.A.*, 23, 33, 33ff.; 51, 516ff. (esp. 516, 15; 517, 5).
[2] See above, p. 118, note 5; Luther accuses Zwingli that he does not take the text of Scripture seriously enough: *Tischr.*, 352, 626.
[3] *W.A.*, 6,508; 511; 26, 462, 1; 38, 264, 26ff.; 54, 434, 14; *de Wette*, V, 567ff., 696ff.; *Tischr.*, 3,793.
[4] (*der Papst*) *sollt das Messer bei dem Stiel fassen, so fasset er's bei der Schneiden. So tun ihm die Schwärmer nicht, die werfen das Messer gar hinweg und sagen, es sei kein Messer. Sic anabaptistae werfen die Taufe gar hinweg. Der Papst, der scheisst mir drein, lässt's sonst eine Taufe bleiben. Schwermerii substantiam adimunt.* . . . *Tischr,*. 342.
[5] *W.A.*, 50, 6ff.

Puritans and super-Protestants who believe that ritual, eucharistic vestments or candles *must* be abolished.[1] Luther is quite prepared to discuss the question whether rich or simple ritual is preferable, and whether a eucharistic vestment is better than a black gown or not.[2] But whenever the attempt is made to abolish "evangelic freedom" in these matters by any kind of Puritan legalism, Luther sees no point in discussing these matters any further. He says that the people he hates most are those who fight against harmless ceremonies and thus establish slavery instead of freedom.[3] It is more necessary to fight against these people than the Pope, for they are more harmful than the Pope.[4] Their attitude in this relatively unimportant sphere of ceremonies shows that their whole religious attitude to the Law and the Gospel and the doctrine of justification is wrong.[5]

In later years some branches of the Lutheran Church established a Union Church together with Calvinists or other Protestants (especially in Prussia, Baden, etc.). Many Lutherans still believe that they have more in common with Calvinists, Methodists, Baptists and other Protestants than with Roman Catholics, and that there is something like a close spiritual relationship between all Protestants in opposition to Rome. I do not want to give my own opinion on this matter, and I know that good theological and historical reasons can be given by those who support this conception. But I am absolutely sure that this could not be supported by Luther's own teaching. It seems certain to me that Luther would have repudiated those Calvinistic Prussian electors and kings, who persecuted Lutheran ceremonies and doctrines, for the benefit of their unionistic Protestant tendencies, more violently than he resisted the Pope.

Why is Luther so sure that his interpretation of the Bible is the only right one and that every diligent and honest reader of the Bible must arrive at his conclusions? There are three possible explanations:

[1] *W.A.*, 18, 123.

[2] *W.A.*, 12, 35ff.; *Tischr.*, 6,006; 6,868.

[3] We must remember that a wrong legalism in Luther's eyes is the worst invention of the devil: "*summa eius (diaboli) ars est, dass er kann ex evangelio legem machen.*" *Tischr.*; 590.

[4] "*Nam magis mihi cum ipsis est bellum quam cum Papa, et magis ipsi nocent. Ego sane nullas ceremonias damno, nisi qui pugnant cum evangelio, ceteras omnes in ecclesia nostra servo integras . . . Sic et missam in solitis vestibus et ritibus celebramus. . . . Summa nullos magis odi, quam eos, qui ceremonias liberas et innoxias exturbant et necessitatem ex libertate faciunt.*" *Briefw.*, March 14th, 1528 (No. 1,239).

[5] Legalists and fanatics (*Schwärmer*) are equally dangerous and their principles are very similar. "*Bei den Schwärmern sind das die besten Prediger, die diese vier Stücke wohl können: Eins, keinen Chorrock anziehen; das Andere, keine Kasel; das Dritte, nichts von der Beichte halten, und zum Vierten, dass im Sakrament des Altars nichts sei denn Brot und Wein*": *Tischr.*, 6,876.

(1) A psychological explanation: Luther believed himself to be specially chosen as God's instrument; but this explanation is insufficient. In this case he would have given theological reasons why people ought to believe more in him than in the Pope and his many followers. He is convinced that God has given him a special task,[1] but he clearly thinks that every individual Christian has the same right as himself to read the Bible and make up his mind on doctrinal questions. Only later generations started speaking of Luther as if he could claim a special revelation from God.

(2) An historical explanation: A doctor who detects a new method of diagnosis for a certain disease may easily think that this new method is infallible. It may be some time before he realises that the new method is definitely better than previous methods, but that it nevertheless still allows for a small number of errors. Luther thus thought he might be able to decide all theological controversies by going back to the Bible and the Early Church. Trusting in this great discovery, it does not occur to him that this new method, while being much superior to previous methods, is not completely safe, and still contains the danger of ambiguous interpretations and different opinions.

(3) A third explanation would claim, quite simply, that in fact Luther *was* right, i.e. that his way of interpreting the Bible is the only possible way, and that all other interpretations either are based on selected Biblical passages only while ignoring other vital parts, or that other interpreters try to read the Bible "in the light of reason," correcting, ignoring or misinterpreting parts of it. There are still many Lutherans who would hold that Luther's teaching is in fact the only interpretation which does *complete* justice to the Bible.

[1] *W.A.*, 10, III, 8, 5; compares himself with Moses, *Tischr.*, 113.

VII
CHURCH AND STATE

1. *Introduction*

"It is true that the teaching of Martin Luther, the father of the Reformation in Germany, gave such emphasis to the rights and God-given powers of the State as to provide rather convenient grounds for State tyranny. But we ought not to forget that it was in Germany that the first Nazi outrages against the Christian religion took place, and that it was Germans who stood up against them."[1]

THERE is a widespread belief that Luther not only conceded to the State and princes the right of doing in the political sphere whatever they liked to do without any regard to Church opinion or Christian principles, but that he even surrendered the whole Church unconditionally to the Princes and the State. Many people imagine Luther as the father of Erastianism,[2] giving the State unlimited power to rule the Church and demanding from the Church the religious deification of the State. Some even allege that it was Luther's outspoken principle to let the State decide the religion of its subjects and to demand that the subjects should obey blindly, according to the principle: *Cuius regio eius religio.* I do not quite see how anyone can hold this opinion in view of the fact that from 1521 to his death (1546) Luther refused obedience to the demands of the Reich Government and Emperor to recant and to stop his reformation activities, and in view of the fact that he never asked his followers under Roman Catholic rule to return to the Roman Catholic Church or even to attend Roman Catholic Mass on the demand of their princes.[3] But, nevertheless, this impression of Luther existed in wide circles, mainly among National Socialists in Germany and the members of Quisling's government in Norway, but also in other circles. It must even be admitted that a similar impression of Luther prevails among large sections of British Christians.

[1] *The Spiritual Issues of the War*, issued by the Religious Division of the Ministry of Information, London, October 2nd, 1941 (No. 100).

[2] Erastianism = supposed doctrine of Erastus (Heidelberg physician of sixteenth century), subordinating ecclesiastical to secular power.

[3] *W.A.*, 38, 88ff.

Those Lutherans, however, who resisted the State dictatorship in Church affairs in Germany and Norway, and who protested against anti-Christian principles in public and political life in these countries and Denmark, had not the slightest feeling of acting in contradiction to Luther. On the contrary, the German Confessional Church, and still more the Norwegian Lutheran bishops and pastors and universities, based their protests expressly on Luther and quoted many passages in his writings in support of the conviction that the Lutheran Church can never be blindly obedient to the State and that any sort of Establishment and co-operation between State and Church must rest on definite conditions and limitations.[1] This interpretation of Luther is also shared by theologians in the other Scandinavian countries, including Finland. Many American and Canadian Lutherans are still more outspoken and think that Luther was a champion in the fight against Erastianism, that he was opposed to any idea of a State Church, and was the only reformer who really tried to "render unto Cæsar the things that are Cæsar's, and unto God the things that are God's," and who in no case rendered the things that are God's to Cæsar.[2]

The whole controversy is a typical illustration of the obvious fact that the various Christian denominations don't know each other very well and accuse one another of those faults which they themselves have in the eyes of the other. There are many Lutherans who believe that the principle *Cuius regio eius religio* was a typical Roman Catholic principle, an outcome of "immoral Jesuit theology"[3] (in fact, it was an outcome neither of Lutheran nor Roman Catholic theology, but a political compromise and working agreement). And there are other Lutherans who believe that the Erastian subjection of the Church to the State is practised in its most extreme form in the Church of England, where a Parliament composed of members belonging to many different religions has to decide on the contents of prayer books, and a Prime Minister can directly influence the appointments of bishops of a Church to which he may not belong. Moreover, the impression was created that the Church of England, in the course of history, frequently changed its attitude under the pressure of succeeding kings and governments, while the Lutheran Church managed to retain her identity even under Roman Catholic rule (Bavaria, Saxony) without the slightest compromise with Roman

---

[1] *Kristen Gemenskap*, Årgång XV, No. 2, Upsala and Stockholm, May, 1942, pp. 70f., 75ff.

[2] Cf. C. F. W. Walther, *Die rechte Gestalt einer vom Staate unabhängigen Evangelisch-Lutherischen Ortsgemeinde*, St. Louis, Mo., 1885.

[3] e.g. A. Müller-Gutenbrunn, *Altoesterreich*, Wien, 1922, pp. 9f.

Catholic doctrine or Church order. Other Lutherans, again, believe that it was Calvin who handed over the control of Church affairs to the secular government (of Geneva) and that similar things happened under Cromwell, while, on the other hand, those English Free Churches which were influenced by Calvin's doctrine managed to keep independent of the State, and not infrequently joined the chorus of those who accuse Luther, not Calvin, of Erastianism.

All these judgments probably contain some small amount of truth, but a greater amount of misunderstanding and half-truth. This ought to make the Lutherans more careful before they criticise other Churches for their Erastianism; but it should also make other Churches more careful not to pronounce on Luther's attitude in this question without adequate knowledge.

If we want to acquire this adequate knowledge, we must not rely on a few individual quotations from Luther which can easily be misunderstood, especially if they are taken out of their context; and there are very many theologians who call themselves Lutherans who give a very one-sided interpretation of Luther's attitude to the State. It is not quite easy to acquire a comprehensive knowledge, as Luther's writings did not include a treatise on the State Church. We have to collect our information from the whole of Luther's writings, for he pronounced on these questions as they arose.[1]

2. *By what power should the Church be governed?*

Nobody can be converted by force, but only by the Word of God. Therefore no external power ought to be used for the purpose of governing the Church and of fighting heresies. Fire and sword are bad means of protecting the Church's integrity. It is against the will of the Holy Spirit to burn heretics. The sword which the Church has to use is the sword of the spirit—"the Word."[2] When the Emperor refers to his duty of protecting the Church by forcibly suppressing heretics, Luther remarks: "This ought to be done by the ministers through the Word, as was done by the Apostles."[3] Consequently, he does not like the habit of the

---

[1] A collection of quotations, J. Meinhold, *"Der Staat in Luthers Verkündigung,"* in *Luther* (quarterly of the *Luthergesesellschaft*), München, 1932, pp. 33-40; 93-100; 1933, pp. 1-12; cf. McKinnon, *op. cit.*, III, 282-96.

[2] *"Haereticos comburi est contra voluntatem spiritus. . . . Christus non voluit vi et igne cogere homines ad fidem. Dedit ob id gladium spiritus, ut in hoc pugnarent, qui sui spiritus filii sunt. At gladium spiritus, quod est verbum dei . . .",* W.A., 7, 139f., esp. lines 14 and 37; cf. 439f.; *"Nollem vi et caede pro Euangelio certari",* Briefw., January 16th, 1521 (*an Spalatin*); cf. W.A., 11, 268, 19; 30, II, 492, 14; Briefw., Nos. 452, 459 465, 1,215.

[3] W.A., 15, 256, 16; cf. W.A., 11, 268, 21.

English King and the German Emperor to bear the title "Defender of the Faith."¹ These principles can be found throughout Luther's life. And while Luther thinks that the Church must retain its right to excommunicate unworthy members, he insists that this excommunication should carry with it no civil disadvantages, and that the person thus excommunicated ought even to be allowed to listen to preaching in church (as this may convert him), but that he should be "driven out" of the church before the celebration of Holy Communion.² And the Bishops ought to govern the Church, not by means of force, but by means of "the Word."³

But is it a practical possibility to take "the Word" as the only "sword" for governing the Church? If there is a minister who spreads heresies, or leads an un-Christian life, he ought to be persuaded by his colleagues, or the theological faculties, or the Bishop or Superintendent, that his way is wrong and that he should repent. But what will happen if he does not repent? Is there some authority in the Church able to dismiss him? We have seen that Luther thinks that it must be possible for the Church to stop the preaching of heretical doctrine in its pulpits and to save the congregation from bad ministers. While no particular form of Church constitution is prescribed by God, the Church must try to arrange for the setting up of some sort of authority (committee, bishop, faculty, synod, etc.) that may pronounce judgment on a heretical minister. But what happens if the guilty minister does not accept this judgment, and continues to preach and live in his vicarage?⁴ It is the same question as exists for the most "disestablished" Free Church: what can be done if a minister or

¹ *W.A.*, 15, 278. 1 and 8.
² *W.A.*, 6, 54, 22ff.; 47, 284f.; *Tischr.*, 3,549; 3,778; 5,438; 5,477; Roman Catholic misuse, *Tischr.*, 6,796. The power bestowed by the office of the "keys" is in the main a spiritual weapon; discipline is kept in Church by the power of the Word, *W.A.*, 17, II, 453, 5; 30, II, 490ff., esp. 492, 18.
³ *W.A.*, 6, 69 (as early as 1520!); cf. Augsbg. Conf., Art. 28; see H. Diem, "*Die Autorität der Kirchenleitung und das vierte Gebot*" in *Evangelische Theologie*, 1937, pp. 379–93; Theodosius v. Harnack, *Die Kirche, ihr Amt, ihr Regiment*, Nürnberg, 1862, pp. 8of.; Thomas Breit, *Bekenntnisgebundenes Kirchenregiment*, Series *Bekennende Kirche*, 5. Reihe, Heft 45, München, 1936; Helmut Gollwitzer, *Amt und "Führertum" in der Kirche*, in *Evangelische Theologie*, 1934–5, p. 112.
⁴ An interesting example: Luther tries to stop "blasphemous" services (Roman Catholic Mass) in Wittenberg Castle Church (*a*) by letters to the responsible canons, i.e. by "the Word" (*Briefw.*, Nos. 586, 634, 648); (*b*) by sermons (*W.A.*, 11, 157ff.; 12, 621ff.; 645ff.; 15, 764ff.); (*c*) when the canons do not yield, Luther threatens them with excommunication by the Christian community in Wittenberg (represented by the Vicar and the Mayor) and with his own resignation if this blasphemy is not discontinued. The Elector interfered by saying he hoped that Luther would refrain from threats and, *as he teaches himself, let the Word of God act in this case* (*Briefw.*, No. 794). But it was obvious that the "Word of God" was not sufficient to stop the "blasphemous" services; cf. McKinnon, *op. cit.*, III, 107ff.

I

Church official wilfully defies the constitution of the Church? Should the congregation leave and found another Church, or should it go to a legal authority set up by the State and ask for protection for its trust deed and constitution, which, of course, may ultimately result in State intervention against the guilty minister? Even the excommunication of laymen may raise similar problems, especially in cases where they hold any Church offices.

Luther saw these implications,[1] but he was not able to make an absolutely clear-cut decision. I wonder whether one can really blame him for this? Many present-day Free Churches have not solved this problem yet, and the legal entanglement between Church and State in Luther's time was much greater than in present-day England or America. If we read Luther's utterances, we feel that he makes a real effort to separate the Church government from any form of external power and secular sword, but that his decisions often seem ambiguous. He always tries to persuade heretics by "the Word," but if this is unsuccessful, and if their heresies become an indirect danger to the State, he does not prevent the State from interfering.[2]

We must not forget that religious struggles very often do have consequences for the State. The fanatics and Anabaptists in Luther's days publicly proclaimed revolution against the State authorities, and in one German town (Munster) the Anabaptists established a State of their own, introducing polygamy and communism, forcing all Christians to be re-baptised, punishing orthodox Christians and publicly defying the Emperor and the Reich constitution. Surely Luther could not deny the right of the State to interfere in such a situation, even if the causes were to some extent religious.[3] In 1535 the State authorities ended this Anabaptist régime by force.

This example shows that some of the "heresies" involved a direct or indirect danger to the State. Luther thought he had to grant to the State the right of protecting its own authority, of suppressing riots, civil war or crime which may have arisen from religious motives. In practice, of course, this very often amounted to suppression of sects and "heretics" by State force, and this unavoidable consequence was bound to create the impression that Luther was only too glad whenever the State forcibly suppressed those heresies which the Church with "the Word" had been unable

---

[1] *W.A.*, 51, 523ff.; 53, 224.
[2] It is the duty of a Church "superintendent": " . . . *ut omnia haec solo verbo tentes et impugnes . . .*", but Luther adds: "*caeterum ad Magistratum pertinet illis interdicere, si quid ferendum ab eis non est. . . .*" *Briefw.*, March 26th, 1522 (to N. Hausmann).
[3] *W.A.*, 31, I, 208, 1; McKinnon, *op. cit.*, IV, 35–75.

to suppress. Luther was not blind to the dangers of the situation, and he knew that the State could very easily misuse its power. Sometimes he feels uneasy about this danger.¹ Who was to decide the question whether the State's interest was or was not involved in a religious dispute? The Lutheran Church had often to cope with this problem in its later history. Some Prussian princes thought it was in the interest of State unity to force Lutherans to compromise with the Presbyterians and to sacrifice some of their beliefs in order to found a Union Church. Those Lutherans who tried to preserve the integrity of the Lutheran Church were persecuted and imprisoned under the pretext that they acted against the unity and interest of the State. Or, to take more recent examples, Quisling's government in Norway thought that the secrecy of confession represented a danger to the State and that therefore the State is entitled to force the Church to abolish this principle; Nazis in general think that it is against the interests of the State if the Christians recognise baptised Jews as brethren and full members of their churches. But is it fair to make Luther responsible for this obvious misuse and misinterpretation of his principles by State authorities? The other alternative would have been to forbid the State to interfere with any action of its citizens for which religious motives are claimed. This conception would have been still more misused and was bound to lead to anarchy and civil war. Progressive Western States try to arrive at a certain compromise by making concessions to the religious conscience under the condition that the security of the State is not really threatened (e.g. tribunals for conscientious objectors, concessions to those who will not take an oath), but the security of the State overrides other considerations. I think Luther's own opinion is not very far from this attitude, and I cannot see that any other reformer has definitely solved this problem.

Some modern States still have a law directed against public blasphemy. Luther thinks that a *Christian* prince has a definite obligation to protect the religious feeling of his subjects and to prevent any kind of public blasphemy which may impress and seduce young and impressionable people. It is not surprising that in his eyes the Roman Mass was such a kind of blasphemy.² He therefore thinks that a Christian prince has a duty to forbid the Roman Mass *in public*. When the Canons of Altenburg refused to stop saying Mass, Luther advises his Elector: they ought to be

---

¹ "*Nam quod vos sperare videmini, ut executio vel per ipsum Principem fiat, valde incertum est, nec vellem politicum magistratum in id officii misceri, sed omnibus modis separari, ut staret vera et certa distinctio utriusque magistratus*": Briefw., June 26th, 1533 (to ministers in Hessen).

² W.A., 6, 497ff.; 8, 477ff.; 18, 8ff.; 38, 195ff.; and many other passages.

allowed to say Mass and to adore "as many Gods as they like" behind closed doors. Nobody must force them to accept Luther's doctrine; they should only be prevented from causing public scandal and from seducing other people. Their personal liberty and property should not be imperilled and they should be allowed to live without persecution, as long as they consent to the above-mentioned limitation, or prove from Holy Scripture that their Mass is *not* a public blasphemy.[1]

Present-day Lutherans would readily admit that this form of "tolerance" was very limited and that it was highly dangerous to presuppose sufficient expert theological knowledge on the part of the State to decide whether or not a particular kind of worship is a blasphemy. What, however, they would not admit is that Luther on this point yielded more power to the State than did other Churches in his time. In England and Scotland and other Protestant countries there was a widespread opinion that the State had to suppress celebrations of the Roman Mass, and Calvin was hardly more "tolerant" than Luther on this point; and Roman Catholic states were just as intolerant of Protestant worship.

But Luther was not even the first to concede these rights to the State. It was the general practice long before his time to ask the State's help against heretics and often even against heretics who were completely harmless to the *State*. If Luther did anything, he tried to *limit* the State's rights in this ecclesiastical sphere. It is especially unfair when Catholics complain that Luther asked the Princes to protect his Church, for we must never forget that it was Luther's Roman Catholic opponents who brought the whole question of Lutheranism before the *State* authorities. Luther's case was investigated at the *Diets*; the Estates of the Realm (princes, governments, etc.) pronounced against him at the request of the Roman Catholics, and these secular authorities were charged with suppressing Lutheranism.[2] If Luther wanted not to sudmit, he was bound to enlist the help of the secular authorities in not carrying out decrees hostile to Lutheranism, and in protecting his Church. The action of his opponents forced him to ask for this protection.

3. *Christ's One Body*

When Luther saw that the Pope and the bishops were not willing to carry out the necessary Church reforms, and that the Pope had even excommunicated him in order to punish him for his reformation activities, he tried to win the help of the *leading*

---

[1] *Briefw.*, February 9th, 1526 (No. 978); cf. McKinnon, *op. cit.*, III, 104ff. *W.A.*, 15, 241ff.; 30, III, 321ff.; Elert, *op. cit.*, I, 327ff.

laymen in the Church to promote the necessary reforms. He issued proclamations asking Christian princes, magistrates, and the nobility in general to help their Church to carry out necessary reforms. He takes this line mainly in 1520 and in the immediately following years.[1] His conception was not based on the opinion that the State, princes or leading laymen *as such* had the right to govern the Church. He emphasises that the Christian congregation is not identical with the civil community.[2] But *Christian* princes and governments had become members of the Body of Christ.[3] The Pope, bishops and clergy may be considered to be the eyes of the Body of Christ; princes and powerful laymen (if they are Christian!) the hands. If the eye suffers, and has not enough strength of its own to defend itself against disease, the hand is allowed and even obliged, to help.[4] This is an emergency measure, "the only remaining remedy."[5] If the Pope and bishops refuse to deal with disease in the Church, Christian princes and powerful laymen ought to help; for Christ has only one Body, not two.[6]

The astonishing thing in the whole conception was the fact that Luther showed such confidence in the sincerity and Christian convictions of the princes and nobility. We are tempted to ask ourselves whether this lack of worldly wisdom was due to his having the mentality of a former monk. We must not forget, however, that Luther had every reason to believe that at least some of the princes and noblemen (e.g. Franz von Sickingen and Ulrich von Hutten) were seriously interested in Church reform.[7] But many of Luther's hopes faded and he very quickly realised that the majority of the princes were in no way sincere Christians nor interested in Luther's Church reform. A few years later we find Luther using most violent expressions against the "madness of the princes,"[8] who "are all robbers,"[9] who "remain princes and never become Christians,"[10] and make a real Christian government in Germany impossible.[11] From now onward, Luther very strictly

---

[1] *W.A.*, 6, 258; 407ff.; establishment of Christian schools (1524), *W.A.*, 15, 27ff.
[2] *W.A.*, 6, 292, 23 and 26.
[3] *W.A.*, 6, 410, 3.
[4] *W.A.*, 6, 409, 12; cf. *W.A.*, 6, 408ff.; 413, 33; 323, 1; 8 679, 24.
[5] *W.A.*, 6, 413, 28; 258, 24.
[6] *W.A.*, 6, 408, 33.
[7] Cf. O. Flake, *Ulrich v. Hutten*, Berlin, 1929; McKinnon, *op. cit.*, III, 159–74.
[8] *W.A.*, 11, 246f.; cf 8, 679, 24; P. Drews, *Entsprach das Staatskirchentum dem Ideale Luthers? Ergänzungsheft zur Zeitschrift für Theologie und Kirche*, Tübingen, 1908, p. 29ff.
[9] *W.A.*, 17, I, 478, 18; 17, II, 40, 28; "... mit Gewalt der armen Kirchen das Brot aus dem Maul reissen"; *W.A.*, 22, 18, 10; *Tischr*, 393, 5,635; 5,663; 6,301; 6,998.
[10] *W.A.*, 11, 246, 23; 15, 255 and 277ff.
[11] *W.A.*, 31, I, 83.

emphasises the distinction between the "two powers," the secular and the ecclesiastical.[1] During 1522–3 he avoids as much as possible basing his reforming activity on the help of secular powers.

4. Congregationalism?

At this period Luther is inclined to organise the Church by giving as much power as possible to the individual local congregation. He explains this point of view in books sent to the Christians at Prague[2] and Leisnig.[3] The local parish congregation should elect a body of men which shall have the right to act in Church affairs. It is not quite certain how far this body at the same time is responsible for the secular affairs of the city. It was very difficult in those times and still later on to distinguish between the members of the local parish *congregations* in a city and the *citizens* of that place. Both were practically identical in a completely Lutheran city. In our day it may happen that in a State election we vote for someone whose politics we trust but with whose religious opinion we may not agree, and in a Church election we may vote for someone who shares our religious opinion, but with whom we may not agree politically. This modern distinction was unthinkable three or four hundred years ago. The voters of a city would elect those representatives whom they trusted both politically and ecclesiastically, and in this way a body of representatives arose who were at the same time a parochial church council and a council of city magistrates. Its chairman was at the same time lay president of the parish church council and mayor of the city. This state of affairs existed in many Lutheran cities for a long time. A definite formation of two separate bodies was effected in many German cities only in the nineteenth century, and survivals— e.g. appointments of church organists by the magistrates—may still be found.

5. Ecclesiola in ecclesia

While Luther always retains the principle that the local congregations should have *some* rights in Church affairs, and while still in 1542 he asks the people representing the congregations of Naumburg diocese to confirm the election of the Bishop,[4] Luther is very quickly aware of great difficulties, preventing him from giving all church rights into the hands of the local parish congregations. If all those who had ever been baptised, but had no

---

[1] A few examples: *W.A.*, 11, 245ff.; 21, 85, 12; 36, 28; 37, 598; 47, 284; 51, 11; *Tischr.*, 5,178; 5,179; 6,234; Drews, *ibid*.
[2] *De instituendis ministris Ecclesiae*, *W.A.*, 12, 169ff.
[3] *W.A.*, 11, 408ff.; 12, 11ff.
[4] Köstlin-Kawerau, *op. cit.*, II, 556; cf. *W.A.*, 53, 257, 21.

knowledge of religion, nor faith in Christ, were allowed to decide the fate of the parish to which they belonged, to elect or even to dismiss the ministers, great disorder was bound to arise.¹ For this reason Luther stresses the point that such rights could only be given to congregations that had respect for Biblical considerations,² or to those members of a congregation who were really believing Christians, and "had the Word."³

As a consequence, he wondered during the following years whether it would not be best to collect from the members of each parish a nucleus of really believing and serious Christians who might form, so to speak, a little church within the big Church. Their names should be entered on a register and all the church affairs of the parish should be regulated by them.⁴ But he is very reluctant to carry this into practice.⁵ He was afraid that the distinction between "real" Christians who bore all responsibility for Church life in the parish, and less perfect Christians who simply were looked after by the Church, was bound to have very bad consequences (sectarian spirit, hypocrisy, etc.). When the Elector of Hessen proposed to draw up a Church constitution on these lines in 1526, Luther prevented him.⁶ Luther's original plan of basing the reconstruction of the church on the full responsibility of the individual local congregation had, to a great extent, failed.

6. "*State Church*"?

In his early years Luther believed strongly in the sound Christian sense of the common people. This belief was shaken, not only by the misuse of democratic rights by many congregations (e.g. Leisnig, Zwickau and Orlamund), but especially through the Peasants' Revolution of 1525. Luther had previously thought that the demands of the peasants who wanted social reforms in Germany were quite reasonable. He thought that the plight of the peasants was deplorable and he often urged influential people to do everything in their power to improve the situation of the peasants. The peasants took this as an encouragement. But Luther warned

---

¹ *Briefw.*, August 11th, 1523; August 19th, 1523; September 30th, 1535; see above, p. 84, note 1; Drews, *Entsprach das Staatskirchentum (op. cit.)*, p. 54.

² *W.A.*, 12, 16, 4; 11, 408ff.

³ *Nam iis, qui credunt, haec scribimus, qui non credunt istis non capiuntur. W.A.*, 12, 192, 25; cf. 12, 193, 36; 12, 195, 4.

⁴ *W.A.*, 19, 75, 3; the examination before admission to the Lord's table a first step in this direction; see above, p. 50, note 3.

⁵ Th. Kolde, "*Luthers Gedanke von der ecclesiola in ecclesia,*" in *Zeitschrift für Kirchengeschichte XIII*, Gotha, 1892, pp. 552ff.; G. Hilbert, *Ecclesiola in ecclesia*, 1924.

⁶ *Briefw.*, January 7th, 1527 (No. 1,071).

them again and again that they should try peaceful negotiations and not unloose the forces of civil war. He agreed that some of the peasants' demands for Church reform were in agreement with the Bible, but that many of their more political demands, although reasonable, could be neither proved nor disproved from Holy Scripture.[1] For those who know Luther's attitude to the Bible it is not surprising that he feared the degradation of "the Word of God" to a handbook of social politics.[2] When the peasants raised their political demands in the name of the Bible and used destruction and force, Luther turned against them.[3] The peasants felt he had betrayed them and he lost his popularity. He, however, thought that he had acted in good faith by refusing to allow his Biblical reformation to be entangled in a political and social struggle.

After the Peasants' War, Luther is horrified by the bare idea of riot and revolution. He thinks that the common man has to a large extent shown his inability to understand the Gospel properly and that therefore *"Herr omnes"* (Mr. Everybody) was not able to carry out the Church Reformation without help from the authorities.[4]

But at the very time of the peasants' revolution, when Luther despaired of the common sense of the common man, he felt more and more the urgent need of reorganising the Church. There were chaotic conditions. We remember that Luther had often enough complained that the Roman Catholic bishops had not done their duty; that they were worldly princes, more given to pleasure and politics than to the work of the Church.[5] But in many places, through the Reformation carried out by Luther's followers, the jurisdiction of the Roman bishops had virtually ceased, and even the slight amount of Church control exercised by them came to an end. In normal times it would have been bad enough if there had been no one to exercise episcopal functions, but it was disastrous in reformation times. Luther's reforming ideas spread through personal contacts, writings, and the activities of his friends; and reforms were carried out without uniform planning. Vicars, Church officials, universities and secular powers, were busily engaged in abolishing what they thought to be abuses in the Church. Much was left to chance, and while reformation was introduced in many places, there were neighbourhoods in which the

[1] *W.A.*, 18, 291–334, esp. 325–8; cf. P. Kingdon, "Church and State in Germany" in *Theology*, Vol. XXXVIII, No. 224, February, 1939, pp. 141f.; R. H. Tawney, *Religion and the Rise of Capitalism*, Pelican Edition, pp. 81ff.
[2] For the whole, cf. Tawney, *ibid.*, pp. 71–87; McKinnon, *op. cit.*, III, 174–210.
[3] *W.A.*, 18, 357–401.
[4] *W.A.*, 18, 71, 10; 22, 143; 28, 678, 18.
[5] e.g. *Bekenntnisschriften*, p. 458.

old Roman Catholic order continued. There were priests who were responsible for two villages and who on the same day had to say Roman Mass in one village and a Lutheran service in the other. It also happened that the Roman Catholic and Lutheran priest officiated in the same parish. Something had to be done to end these chaotic conditions and to organise the reformation activities with some amount of uniformity.

Luther thought that this could best be done by small committees, consisting of theologians and lawyers formed in close touch with Wittenberg University. These Committees went from parish to parish examining the state of affairs and giving instruction, and, if necessary, ordering vicars and Church officials to establish "Gospel" preaching and orderly Church conditions in every parish. Much was done to try and remedy the immorality and ignorance of the clergy, and to protect Church property against greedy noblemen.

These committees were called *visitatores*; but it was obvious that these Visitors had no authority whatever if they came in a private capacity. They had to be authorised by the prince of each territory concerned. For this reason, Luther approaches his own Prince and asks him for such authorisation. He is very careful to explain to the Prince that he has no Church rights as such and emphasises that it is *not* the task of the secular powers to control religious teaching or to govern the Church.[1] But Luther's Prince was a member of the Christian Church and, as a good Christian Prince, should wish to help in the reorganising of his Church. Moreover, the present conditions being so chaotic, riots and disorder were involved, even for the State. As it was only the Prince who had the *power* to help, Luther, in the name of the Church, asked him to use his power and to authorise his committees of Visitors. This was the first fateful step leading to many consequences.[2]

But this was not the only occasion on which Luther asked the Prince's help. Many questions of Church organisation arose in the following years, and Luther and his friends proposed measures and always asked the Prince to authorise their schemes. In this way Luther was convinced that the Church actually was governed by the best Christian experts of the country, i.e. by himself, by the University of Wittenberg, by committees of theologians and lawyers, by Bugenhagen, the Vicar of Wittenberg (being practically the first priest of the country, as Wittenberg

[1] *W.A.*, 26, 200, 28; cf. next note.

[2] *Briefw.*, October 31st, 1525 and November 30th, 1525 (to Elector Johann); February 9th, 1526 (about the Canons of Altenburg); *W.A.*, 26, 197, 19ff.; cf. K. Holl, *op. cit.*, pp. 360–80.

was the capital), and that the Prince was only assisting his Church by enabling these churchmen to do their work. This same system was copied in other territories.

While Luther was at the beginning honestly convinced that this system allowed the Church to be governed by Church people according to Church principles, it was a temptation for the princes, and they themselves could easily look upon it from a different angle. They may have felt that they were governing the Church and Luther and his friends were only their advisers. This danger was not so great while Luther was alive and his authority unchallenged. And yet there were occasions on which the princes refused to authorise measures proposed by Luther, and issued Church laws on their own authority.[1] In the later years of his life, Luther became more and more suspicious of the intentions of the princes. He may rightly have suspected that many princes were only waiting for his death in order to rule the Church according to their own ideas. Luther tried to counteract the possibility of this development by supporting the appointment of Lutheran bishops or superintendents who would defend the spiritual freedom of the Church. As a matter of fact, the leading clergy later on proved an obstacle to the Erastian plans of many princes who tried therefore to limit their influence or even to abolish their office. I think Th. Kaftan is not wrong when he says that these unfortunate relations between Church and State in Germany "developed out of Luther's measures, but against Luther's will."[2] It is very probable that Luther would have taken stronger action against this development if he had lived longer, and even after his time there have been many Lutherans who tried to remedy this fault. But it is hardly fair to say that the Lutheran Church in Germany was a State Church in the present-day meaning of the term.[3] In order to clarify Luther's position more fully, we have to add a few notes.

7. *Emergency bishops*

It is evident that Luther considers the princes' share in Church administration to be temporary only for the time of the special "emergency." He calls the princes "emergency bishops, as no

[1] In fact, the "visitors" were dependent on the authority given to them by the prince. *Briefw.*, Nos. 1,371; 1,394; 1,396; 1,397; 1,508; 1,519; cf. K. Holl, *op. cit.*, pp. 372–5.
[2] Th. Kaftan, *Erlebnisse und Betrachtungen des ehemaligen Generalsuperintendenten von Schleswig*, Kiel, 1924, p. 278.
[3] Cf. H. H. Kramm, "Organisation and Constitution of the German Protestant Churches" in *Church Quarterly Review*, Vol. CXXXVIII, No. 275 (1944), pp. 87ff.

other bishop wants to help us."[1] This conception, of course, includes the supposition that these "episcopal" functions of the princes must disappear the moment the state of acute emergency ceased to exist. That was not done, and that was one of the chief reasons why Luther's measures had consequences which were contradictory to his own will.

8. The "Christian member"

Previous quotations ought to have shown that Luther does not concede any Church rights to the princes as such, or even to the State,[2] but only to those princes who are "Christian members," so to speak, to the first laymen of the Church. Luther says clearly that only those Princes can co-operate in Church government who are inclined to promote the "pure" Gospel.[3] Since 1530 only those princes or city magistrates who had signed the Augsburg Confession could take a share in the administration of the Lutheran Church. And for Luther this is not only a matter of a formal signature, but should denote real Christian conviction. Roman Catholic princes, or even the Roman Catholic Emperor, have no right to interfere with the Lutheran Church.[4]

Luther takes great care to explain that the Christian must not obey if the prince or the State demand anything contrary to the Christian conscience.[5] They must not recognise an heretic bishop "even though Emperor, Kings, Pope and all devils ordered and demanded it."[6] If the Government orders all heads of households to read a proclamation against Lutheranism to the members and servants of their households, the former may obey the order, but only on condition that they at the same time announce their own adherence to Lutheranism, thus contradicting the Government publicly before the household.[7]

But even those Christian princes who, in Luther's eyes, may be allowed to co-operate in Church administration, are subject to certain limitations. Their co-operation must have been desired by the leading representatives of the Church[8] and they must never

---

[1] Briefw., March 19th, 1539; March 25th, 1539; Tischr., 4,561; W.A., 53, 25ff.; Kawerau in W.A., 12, 8.
[2] J. Meinhold, op. cit., 1932, pp. 93ff.; W.A., 11, 265, 28f.; 7, 284ff.
[3] W.A., 49, 305, 17.
[4] W.A., 51, 534, 30ff.; 34, II, 466ff., esp. 467, 26; 49, 143ff.; P. Drews, Entsprach das Staatskirchentum . . . (op. cit.).
[5] W.A., 15, 241ff.; 39, II, 34ff.; 49, 143, 31ff.
[6] W.A., 53, 246, 24; cf. W.A., 11, 408, 31; "Denn wider Gott hält kein Siegel, Recht, Brauch, noch Obrigkeit," Briefw., May 8th, 1522 (No. 485).
[7] Briefw., No. 1,987 (1532?).
[8] " . . . durch uns und durch die Not selbst, als gewisslich von Gott gebeten und gefordert," Briefw., No. 937; " . . . haben ır . . . demütiglich mit Bitten angelanget den . . . Fürsten," W.A., 26, 197, 19.

use their rights in contradiction to the principles of the Church. When Luther's Prince gives orders in connection with religious questions which in Luther's view are un-Christian, he admonishes the congregation from the pulpit not to obey, explaining that the Prince has gone beyond the limits of his rights.[1] Church assemblies are not dependent on the consent of princes and magistrates, though those are allowed to help if they like.[2]

9. *Is the term "State Church" defensible?*

A strong co-operation between Church and State existed long before Luther's time. Luther himself underlines the fact that there are many examples since the time of Emperor Constantine proving that the Church has again and again accepted help from princes in order to bring about necessary improvements, and that this was always considered to be defensible under certain conditions.[3] Moreover, there is not the slightest doubt that there was a close connection between Church and State government in many places during the Middle Ages, especially in the time preceding the Reformation. Many princes and city magistrates acted as if they were "Popes in their own territory,"[4] and the ecclesiastical conscience was only saved by the theory that these rights were granted by special licence of the Church and could be cancelled by the Church. But Luther did not go beyond this conception. The "State" as such has, in his eyes, no rights at all in Church affairs; only a Christian prince or Christian government can be given these rights. It would perhaps be more correct to describe this state of affairs not by the term "State Church," but by a term like "Federation Church" or "Concordat Church"; this would mean that the Church and the Christian government of a country concluded a federation or concordat, which gave to the Christian prince or government, under certain conditions, certain limited rights and duties in the administration of the Church, while it gave to the Church, under certain conditions, certain rights and duties in the sphere of the State (e.g. financial advantages, influence in schools and universities, etc.).

[1] *Briefw.*, No. 634.
[2] *Briefw.*, November 27th, 1535 (No. 2,274): contradiction to Art. XXI of the Church of England?
[3] e.g. *W.A.*, 26, 300, 31; 50, 522, 30f.
[4] E. Sehling, *Geschichte der protestantischen Kirchenverfassung*, Leipzig, 1907, pp. 9–11. Albert Werminghoff, *Geschichte der Kirchenverfassung Deutschlands im Mittelalter*, I. Band, Hanover and Leipzig, 1905, pp. 247ff.; 261ff.; 269ff. Albert Werminghoff, *National-Kirchliche Bestrebungen im Deutschen Mittelalter*, Stuttgart, 1910, esp. pp. 110ff. Möller-Kawerau, *Lehrbuch der Kirchengeschichte*, III. Band, Freiburg, 1899, p. 68ff. Elert, *op. cit.*, I, pp. 330f. Luther refers to the fact that in his time the bishops of some dioceses (Hildesheim, Lüttich, Utrecht) are practically appointed by secular princes or the Emperor, *Tischr.*, 3,796.

10. *Religious unity within a territory?*

Luther and his opponents both agreed that it would be highly dangerous to have Lutheran and Roman Catholic Churches side by side in the same place. They thought this was bound to lead to constant rivalries, riots, and tumults.[1] Individual tolerance was still outside the imagination in those days. As a matter of fact a few attempts were made to tolerate both Lutherans and Roman Catholics in the same city—sometimes it worked out more peacefully than Luther anticipated. On the other hand, there were many instances when Lutherans and Roman Catholics (or Lutherans and Calvinists) could not live peaceably together. In his later years Luther becomes increasingly afraid of riots and revolutions, caused by religious controversies.[2] He tries to make all Christian princes see that Lutheranism is the right interpretation of Christianity. He demanded very forcibly that every single Christian must have the legal right to live as a Lutheran—to worship God according to the pure Gospel. But in territories where there was no hope of this right, Luther advises his followers to consider the possibility of emigration rather than be the cause of constant friction.[3] Many Lutherans acted in accordance with this advice in the course of history; even up to the nineteenth century, quite a number of them emigrated from Germany to America rather than remain where the official Church had compromised with Calvinism and Rationalism. Some of those, however, who did not emigrate availed themselves of the religious tolerance of those times and formed Lutheran Free Churches in Prussia and elsewhere side by side with the official Church.

11. *Cuius regio, eius religio*

The principle *Cuius regio, eius religio* (the Prince decides the religion of his country) was introduced by the Peace of Augsburg, 1555. Originally, both the Roman Catholics and the Lutherans had claimed that they were the original Catholic Christian Church and that they, therefore, should be recognised as the only official Church of Germany. The Lutherans tried to prove that the Pope had introduced alterations and innovations and therefore excluded himself from the true Catholic Church,[4] while the Roman Catholics alleged the same of Luther. After a period of civil war the Roman Catholics saw that they could not reconquer the whole of

---

[1] *W.A.*, 19, 436ff.; *Briefw.*, No. 978.
[2] *W.A.*, 28, 475, 20; 33, 359, 2.
[3] *Briefw.*, Nos. 1,954; 2,009; *W.A.*, 38, 88ff.
[4] Luther's opinion: The Pope "*hat sich also selbst ausgedreht,*" *W.A.*, 50, 514.

Germany in spite of their original intention to do so. But also the Lutherans saw that they would not win over the whole of Germany to their cause as they had planned. Thus both parties were ready for compromise. The Emperor and the higher authorities of the Reich, therefore, refrained from deciding which of the two parties was the original Christian Church, but recognised both. This compromise resulted in a plan to divide up Germany peacefully between the two denominations. But how could this division be carried out? We have seen that the modern principle that every individual has to decide which religion he will adhere to seemed impracticable to either side. It was thought in 1555 that the only way out was to divide up Germany into purely Lutheran and purely Roman Catholic territories. Most territories having no democratic constitution, it was not possible to let the population vote which should be the denomination of each territory (except in certain cities which had introduced Lutheranism in a democratic way by electing a Lutheran majority in the city government). And so it was resolved that the prince should decide the religion of his territory. That this, on principle, was a specially desirable state of affairs in the eyes of the Lutherans cannot be proved; with equal right one could say that *"cuius regio, eius religio"* was a Roman Catholic principle; for it was sanctioned by the Roman Catholic Emperor and princes, but in reality it was nothing more than a compromise and working agreement and cannot be regarded as a typical outcome either of Lutheran or of Roman Catholic theology.

There was, after all, a certain amount of individual tolerance. Those who would not accept the religion of the territory in which they lived were allowed to emigrate with all their property, and to settle in one of those states which had their religion. Compared with our present time, this shows an astonishing degree of tolerance; for nowadays those who want to leave a state for the sake of their religious or political conviction are very often prevented from doing so, or must give up most of their property before leaving, and very often they are not allowed to immigrate into those states in which they want to live.[1]

The religious Peace of Augsburg was concluded nine years after Luther's death, and therefore we cannot know for certain how he himself would have judged the principle, *Cuius regio, eius religio.*

12. *Religion and politics*

Many people admit that Luther tried to preserve a certain amount of *religious* freedom for the *Church,* but they are con-

[1] Cf. McKinnon, *op. cit.,* IV, 217ff.

vinced that he surrendered the sphere of *politics* unconditionally to the *State*.¹ Luther is accused of failing to apply Christian principles to the world in general—to politics, economics, social questions, education, law and State morals. Even a conference of Lutheran bishops proclaimed in 1939:²

"The Evangelical Church has been taught by Martin Luther to distinguish clearly between the domains of reason and faith, of politics and religion, of State and Church."

But the matter is not as simple as that. We have seen that Luther felt free to make very strong criticisms about the personalities and actions of the princes and the Emperor, and that in certain circumstances he asks his followers to refuse obedience to them. These criticisms are in no way limited to the Princes' attitude to religion and Church affairs; they include strong condemnation of their political actions as well,³ and there are innumerable passages in Luther's writings where he deals with secular and political matters; for, if a matter is admittedly political or secular, it does not mean that the Church is no longer concerned with it.

Luther considers matrimony to be a secular thing subject to secular authority,⁴ and yet he interferes again and again in questions of matrimonial law (including divorce cases) to safeguard the interests of the Church. Even secular and political affairs are not wholly unconnected with the Bible, and he deduces his opinion on matrimonial questions from his study of it, avoiding, however, a narrow legalistic interpretation.⁵

Biblical considerations guide Luther also in his attitude to many other secular things. In his writings, he discussed the rights and duties of governments and the question to what extent

---

[1] Cf. P. Kingdon, *op. cit.*, pp. 141ff. and in *The Modern Churchman*, Vol. XXV, Year No. 10, January, 1936, pp. 559ff.

[2] D. F. Buxton, *Christendom on Trial* (*op. cit.*), p. 21.

[3] He makes public and criticises crimes planned by princes, *Briefw.*, February 12th, 1536(?) (No. 2,297); *W.A.*, 19, 252ff.; 23, 390ff.

[4] *Bekenntnisschriften*, p. 529; the words "natural" and "reason," *W.A.*, 6, 411, 13; 11, 279f.; cf. *W.A.*, 30, III, 74, 2.

[5] *W.A.*, 10, II, 263ff.; 275ff.; 30, III, 198ff.; 207ff. As *examples*: in his letters during a few years: *Briefw.*, No. 722; The following numbers of *one* volume only of the *Briefwechsel* edition (vol. 4) speak about judgments in matrimonial questions: Nos. 1,048; 1,056; 1,057; 1,062; 1,069; 1,134; (divorce in the case of dangerous illness?) 1,211; 1,216; 1,237; 1,245; 1,250; 1,320; 1,327; 1,353; 1,358; 1,361; 1,368. It would be easy to show a similar number in the other volumes. Cf. *Briefw.*, Nos. 1,523; 1,525; 1,526 (Luther threatens to declare a man free by divorce in certain circumstances); thus Luther acts as judge in these questions). Cf. "*iuxta legem Mosi*," No. 1,891; cf. 2,171; *Tischr.*, 4,844; 5,442: meaning what is allowed by Moses cannot be forbidden by God. *W.A.*, 53, 190ff. (Philipp v. Hessen); cf. *Briefw.*, No. 1,056.

a Christian is bound to obey the State.[1] He writes of the problem: under what circumstances is a Christian allowed to do military service, and when is he bound to refuse to take part in war in spite of the orders of the State?[2] He considers at great length the status of the universities and schools and what claims the Church should put forward with regard to them.[3] He gives his opinion on beggars,[4] public morals, riots, drinking and licensing hours.[5] He is very much interested in the foreign political situation, especially in the defence of Europe against the Turks; he thinks that it is the task of the Church to inform Christians on the Turkish atrocities, and on the probable consequences of the Turkish victory on culture and religion.[6] He even interferes in economic questions, and it is surprising to see how often he writes about foreign trade, usury, banking, rents and finance.[7] His various pamphlets on the Ten Commandments deal with many questions which are connected with the State and politics. And in dealing with all these problems Luther does not write in a private capacity as an expert, but as a man of God who has to put forward certain claims of the Church in these matters.[8]

But Luther says quite openly that, under certain conditions and limitations, a preacher has the right to criticise the government.[9] He rebukes the princes and lords because they dislike such criticism and want to rid themselves of Christian critics.[10] But God demands that the Church should criticise as the Prophet Jonah did.[11]

Luther goes even so far as to apply Biblical arguments to the point whether Christians may resist the Emperor if he tries to persecute Lutheranism by force.[12] The Emperor is breaking his baptismal vow if he persecutes "the Gospel," and everybody who

[1] *W.A.*, 11, 245ff.; 261ff.
[2] *W.A.*, 19, 616ff., esp. 656f.; cf. *W.A.*, 6, 265.
[3] *W.A.*, 6, 457ff.; 15, 9ff.; 27ff.; 30, II, 508ff.; *Bekenntnisschriften*, p. 505; *Tischr.*, 4,033; 5,557; 5,603.
[4] *W.A.*, 6, 450, 22; 26, 634ff.
[5] *Briefw.*, Nos. 312; 313; 315; 1,129; 1,158.
[6] *W.A.*, 30, II, 81ff.; 107ff.; 149ff.; 51, 577ff.; *Briefw.*, No. 125.
[7] *W.A.*, 6,466; cf. *W.A.*, 15, 279ff.; 6, 1ff.; 33ff.; *Briefw.*, No. 3,319; *W.A.*, 51, 325ff.; *Briefw.*, 674 *Tischr.*, 3,512; 3,683; 4,863; 4,875; 5,216; 5,429; 5,438; 5,593; 6,576.
[8] Theological and Biblical arguments on political questions: *Briefw.*, Nos. 1,011; 1,258; against destruction of houses, *Briefw.*, Nos. 1,548; imprisonment of the Duke of Braunschweig, *W.A.*, 54, 389ff.; political advice, *Briefw.*, Nos. 1,260; 1,424.
[9] *Tischr.*, 5,258; 6,591; limitation, 181.
[10] *W.A.*, 14, 45f., esp. 14, 46, 4.
[11] *W.A.*, 19, 195, 13; people guilty of usury ought to be excommunicated, *Tischr.*, 5,216, 5,438, 5,593. Luther excommunicates one of them, *Tischr.*, 4,073.
[12] *W.A.*, 30, III, 256ff.; *Briefw.*, No. 1,536 (Vol. V, pp. 249ff.); No. 1,796.

helps him does the same.¹ Thus Luther demands a passive resistance or at least a "non-co-operation." Whether he would have approved of armed resistance is a disputed question. In general he is against every kind of armed revolution by Christians against their government.² On the other hand, at the end of his life he seems inclined to allow his followers to fight a war against their Emperor in defence of their faith, provided that such a war is sanctioned by the Lutheran Princes. One year after Luther's death the Lutheran states took up arms against the Emperor, who tried to suppress their religion and, after a number of conflicts and defeats, forced the Emperor to recognise their religion. It is obvious that the whole idea of armed resistance against the government is disliked by Luther, but all his life he was very certain that a Christian must refuse obedience if the government demands something contrary to the Christian conscience.³

How can this political activity of Luther's be reconciled with his many other utterances demanding a clear separation between secular and spiritual power, between the State and the Church? How can it be reconciled with his attitude to the Peasants' Revolution, when he definitely refused to use the Bible as a handbook for social reforms? We have to admit that it is not quite easy to answer these questions without detailed argument. I personally am convinced that his attitude to politics is much the same as his attitude to Church constitution and ceremonies; some of which are governed by biblical considerations while others are left to the best human discretion (see above, pp. 91ff.). The Christian has to live in this world according to certain principles. Religious doctrine and ethics are closely connected. He must therefore demand from the State freedom which enables him to live according to these principles. If the State refuses to let him do this, he must not submit, and a conflict is unavoidable. In this way, ethics are not the private affair of the individual Christian only, but have a certain effect upon the relations of a Christian, not only to his fellow Christians, but to his neighbours in general, and finally to the State. We have to remember here what we said about the first use of the law (see above, p. 60). While the State as such cannot easily be Christian in the sense of a Church, there are nevertheless certain principles which *every* State must adhere to and certain mistakes which it must avoid if Christians are to live in it without friction; and Christians have the moral right to demand these conditions and the Church has the right to support

[1] *W.A.*, 30, III, 299ff.
[2] The individual Christian has only the alternative of suffering or emigrating. cf. Elert, *op. cit.*, II, 373ff.
[3] Elert, *ibid*.

this demand by public preaching and writing if it happens to be a State whose governing authorities claim to be Christian or to tolerate Christians. It is much more difficult in a State whose government is clearly anti-Christian (e.g. the Turks). If the Christians cannot obtain their conditions, there is probably no other choice left but suffering or emigration.

While there are many political matters which in this way have a direct or indirect relevance to the Bible and the Christian faith, there are other things which definitely belong to the sphere of this world and which can be regulated according to expert knowledge and the best human understanding, e.g. by "the princes, lawyers and reason." I think this distinction became very clear when Luther was asked for his advice in drawing up a constitution for the city of Erfurt. He gives a detailed reply, making it clear in which parts of the constitution he was interested as a man of the Christian Church, which parts he would only recommend as good and useful, and which parts he would leave to the experts because they did not involve any Christian principles.[1]

In this way Luther really arrives at definite Christian claims in the field of politics, and at a system of social ethics. Space does not allow me to say more about this subject, but there is some recent literature dealing with it.[2] When we consider all this, we do not find it astonishing that present-day Lutherans are accused by Fascist States of interfering in politics, while they themselves are convinced that the German and Norwegian Church conflicts were being fought for the very reason of keeping politics out of the Church; on the other hand, however, when Luther is criticised for leaving all political questions completely to the secular authorities, present-day Lutherans usually emphasise that, on the contrary, Luther took a great interest in the problems of this world. Both statements are true.

And yet Luther dislikes all confusion of spiritual and political power.[3] Many bishops had assumed secular rights and functions, had (since the tenth century) acted as princes and administered the state government, organised wars and had the civil legislation and jurisdiction in their hands. Luther thinks that these secular functions should properly be restored to the *secular* princes. This, however, should not lead to the false conclusion that, as a matter of principle, the *ecclesiastical* rights of the bishops, too, should be handed over to the princes. The bishops should keep them if they were prepared to accept "the Gospel"; if the princes took

---

[1] *W.A.*, 18, 536, 29.

[2] W. Betcke, *Luthers Sozialethik*, Gütersloh, 1934.

[3] *Tischr.*, 6,234; 4,635; *W.A.*, 6,430, 5; 433, 26; 11, 271; and the quotations about the separation of secular and spiritual power.

CHURCH AND STATE 147

them over, they only acted as temporary stewards for the bishops during the state of emergency. This handing over of secular power to the princes does certainly *not* mean that the Church is quite uninterested in political and secular affairs.

13. Anti-Semitism?

In our time many attempts are made to describe Luther as the father of modern anti-Semitism. Quotations are given in which he most violently attacks the Jews, but these quotations are very often torn out of their context.

His only accusation against the Jews was that they did not accept Christ. In the first period of his life he blamed the depraved type of Christianity in the Roman Church and its hostile treatment of the Jews as being responsible for their refusal to accept Christ. He wants those Churches that accepted his Reformation to show more kindness to the Jews and he hopes that this would cause the conversion of many of them.[1] His hopes were disappointed; but in spite of this, he never abandoned his original intention of converting the Jews. In the course of time he grows more bitter and disillusioned about his failure. But even in the letter, which for the first time contains rather hard words against the obstinacy of the Jews, Luther emphasises that he wants to preserve his intention of treating the Jews kindly in order to bring them to "their Messiah." He writes to an important Jew, whom he calls "my good friend," telling him that he wants to be the Prophet of the Jews who will convert them. He will treat them well for the "crucified Jew's sake." But his kindness will not be weakness, encouraging the Jews in their resistance to Christ. If they misuse his kind treatment he will change his methods.[2]

This fundamental opinion is still to be found in his writings during the following years, but his tone grew more violent, at times as violent as against the Pope and the Turks. He even demanded far-reaching restrictions for the Jews.[3] His motive is disappointment. The reformation and the kinder treatment of the Jews by Lutherans has not brought about the expected results. On the other hand, the greater freedom which the Jews thus gained was occasionally used by them for religious propaganda among Christians which seems to have had some success. Therefore their religious obduracy and propaganda must be stopped by severe measures. Towards the end of his life he grows more moderate

---

[1] *W.A.*, 11, 314ff. For the whole, cf. McKinnon, *op. cit.*, IV, 192–204.
[2] *Briefw.*, June 11th, 1537.
[3] *W.A.*, 50, 309f.; 31 2ff.; 53, 412ff.; 573ff.

in tone when he writes of the Jews,[1] and during his last sermons in Eisleben, immediately before his death, he demanded again from the pulpit that the Christian faith should be offered to the Jews and that they should be treated kindly if they so deserved.[2]

Whatever we think of Luther's attitude, it had nothing whatever to do with anti-*Semitism*. There was no hostility whatever against people of *Semitic blood* or *race*. The whole conception of races in the modern nationalistic sense was quite alien, not only to Luther, but to his time. For Luther it is a *religious* question only. The bad qualities which he ascribes to the Jews are in his eyes closely connected with their wrong faith. If a Jew is sincerely converted to Christ and accepted into the Church by baptism, he is as genuine a Christian as the Apostles, who themselves were converted Jews.[3] Christ is their cousin "according to blood" and those Jews who drop their antagonism to Christ, and are converted and baptised, are as fully members of the Church as it is possible to be. If some Nazis claim that Luther would approve of measures restricting the rights of baptised Jews within the *German* Church, this is sheer fantasy. He never makes proposals to organise the Church on nationalistic or racial bases. All true believers in one place, whatever their nationality or origin, can be full members of the Church of that place.[4] Luther himself devises a ritual for the baptism of a Jewish girl.[5]

In modern terminology there is constantly a confusion between anti-*Semitism* (objection to so-called *"Semitic"* races) and anti-*Judaism* (objection to the *Jews'* religion). While Luther was young, the greatest propaganda against the Jews' religion, the Talmud and their other sacred writings, was carried on by a *Semite* (if I may use this rather controversial expression), the baptised Jew, Pfefferkorn. And all Luther's writings about the Jews do not raise the slightest *"racial"* questions.[6] It is much more the problem of *religious* intolerance to non-Christian creeds.

I personally (and many modern Lutherans) would, of course, not approve of the intolerant methods and the violent language used by Luther in his writings on the adherents to the Jewish

---

[1] *W.A.*, 54, 16ff.

[2] *W.A.*, 51, 195f.

[3] *W.A.*, 11, 315, 19; *Briefw.*, No. 629, June(?), 1523, to the baptised Jew, Bernhard.

[4] Like Matthias Flacius Illyricus from Istria, who was one of the leaders and held various important offices in the German Lutheran Church in the time of the Reformation.

[5] *Briefw.*, July 9th, 1530 (No. 1,632).

[6] Cf. Luther's high esteem for the *Old* Testament. He thinks that the Jewish prophets like Jeremiah have written against "the Jews" in favour of the Christians, e.g. *W.A.* 20, 569, 27.

faith.[1] But we think that it is deeply unfair to accuse Luther *in a special way* of this intolerance that was quite common in his time. In the Press and literature of recent years the impression is very often given that the medieval world was completely democratic, tolerant on religious questions and kind to the Jews, and that the Church was completely "free of the State" when suddenly Luther appeared and introduced despotism, intolerance, anti-Semitism and Erastianism. It is very difficult *not* to regard such articles as merely political propaganda. At that time there was no tolerance between the Christian denominations anywhere and certainly no tolerance on the part of the Christians towards non-Christian religions. It was only over 200 years later that the German poet Lessing fought for tolerance towards Jews and Mohammedans. It cannot be denied that Luther was very suspicious of other religions. He had found through experience that some Christian sects like the Anabaptists and Fanatics (*Schwärmer*) constituted a real danger for Christian countries and that the Turks threatened the very existence of Christianity in Europe. No wonder that he was over-suspicious of the only other non-Christian religion which, apart from the Turks, he knew of in Europe—namely, the Jews—and that he imagined dangers which did not exist. But other Churches maintained the same fantastic suspicions of the Jews and, as we have to remember, even the Roman Catholic Church was not free of this suspicion, so that Luther accused this Church of its lack of understanding of the Jews.

On the other hand, Luther never forgot that nobody can be convinced of the Christian faith except through the "Word." Where he advocates the use of force against other religions, he wants to protect the State against real or fictitious dangers and he wants Christian Princes to protect their countries against public propaganda on the part of "sects," "heretics," and "wrong religion." But this was in itself a negative protection only; the positive force that would overcome all these dangers was Christian faith. And this can only be created by the means of Word and Sacrament, used by the Holy Spirit as instruments in order to work faith where and when it pleases God.[2]

14. *Conclusion*

Luther apparently thinks that the relations between Church and State cannot be ordered by a fixed rule once for all; because

[1] Cf. letter to *The Times* from the Conference of Lutheran Pastors of German-speaking Congregations (in Great Britain), January 2nd, 1943.
[2] Augsbg. Conf., Art. V.

the Church has not to deal with an "ideal State," but with the varying forms of the existing States in various times and places. The aims of the Church are fixed. How far the Church can work for these aims in co-operation with the State, in separation from it, or how the Church can pursue these aims in conflict with the State, depends on the structure of the State in question. It will, however, not be possible that State and Church ignore each other completely, as there are spheres of life in which their interests are overlapping (e.g. questions of schools, universities, freedom for Christian worship, public holidays, etc.). It will be interesting to observe how the Lutheran Churches in many countries will put these principles of Luther into practice when they are faced with the task of re-ordering their relations with the State after the war.

INDEX

ABSOLUTION, 55, 57–8, 84f.
Adam. *See* Man.
Adiaphoron, 93f., 99–101, 109
Anabaptists, 13, 31, 123f., 130, 149
Anglican Church, 45f., 54, 127f.
Anti-Semitism, 147–9
Apostolic succession, 70–2, 74–7, 90, 106. *See also* ordination.
Aristotle and Plato, 38, 54f.
Atonement, 46f.
Augsburg Confession, 14ff., 139
  Apologia of, 15, 55
Augsburg Peace, 1555, 15, 141f.

BAPTISM, 56f.
  infant baptism, 51, 55, 123
Bible, 105–25
  interpretation of, 120–5
Bishops, 85–7
  Roman Catholic, 29, 132f., 136, 138f., 146f.
  Lutheran, 87–91, 138f., 146f.

CALVIN, JOHANN, 29, 128, 132
Calvinists, 16, 45f., 66, 73, 100, 124
Catechisms, Luther's, 16, 50
Catholic, 122, 141
Celibacy. *See* Matrimony.
Ceremonies. *See* Ritual.
Christ:
  (1) Natures of, 44ff.
  (2) Person of, 44–6
  (3) Work of, 46–9
Church, the, 68ff. (*see also* Catholic):
  (1) *Ecclesiola in ecclesia*, 134f.
  (2) Separations and reunion, 45f., 54f., 72–4
  (3) State Church, 126–8, 135ff., 140–2
  (4) Visible and invisible, 68–70
Church Conflict, German (after 1933), 16, 92f., 127
  Norwegian, 127, 131
Church constitution, 73, 88–9, 90–6, 105, 132–5
  Government, 128–34
Cicero, 37, 104
Communion, Holy, 45f., 53, 55f., 58–9. *See also* Sacraments.
Confession. *See* Absolution.
Confirmation, episcopal, 39f., 51, 69
  Lutheran, 50f.
Congregationalism, 134
Conscientious objection. *See* War.
Consubstantiation. *See* Holy Communion and Sacraments.
Copernicus, 46, 120

Creation, 34ff.
  Ordinances of, 42f.
Creeds, 15, 44

DENMARK, 15, 87, 89, 127
Devil, 41, 47, 102
Doctrine, 70, 72ff., 74–7, 120–5
Donatism, 76

ENTHUSIASTS. *See* Schwärmer.
Erasmus, 20f., 39
Eschatology, 102–4
Ethics. *See* Law.
Eucharistic sacrifice. *See* Mass, Roman.
Eve. *See* Man.
Examination. *See* Ministry.
Excommunication, 129

FAITH, 49
  historic faith, 49–51
  saving faith, 51–2
Fanatics. *See* Schwärmer.
Finance. *See* Property of the Church.
Finitum et infinitum, 52
Finland, 87, 89
Formula of Concord, 16
Free will, 39–41, 68f.

GALATIANS, 24
God, hidden and revealed, 41
  Right Hand of. *See* Heaven.
Government. *See* Princes and State.

HEAVEN, 45f.
High German, 18f.
Holy Spirit, 39, 68f., 70
Humanism, 20f.
Hus, Johann, 30

INDULGENCES, 25f.

JAMES, EPISTLE OF, 111f.
Justification, 22–5, 26f., 47–9. *See also* Faith.
  Forensic, 48f.

KARLSTADT, ANDREAS, 31f., 78

LANGUAGES, classical, 20, 97. *See also* High German.
Lapse, 35ff.
Law, 62–7
  and Gospel, 59–62, 66f., 120f.
  three uses of, 59–62
Lawyers, 21, 146
Liturgy. *See* Ritual.

INDEX

Lutheran, Luther and the Lutherans, 13–18
  the term Lutheran, 14–18, 122

MAN, NATURE OF, 34–43
  original state of, 34f.
Mass, Roman, 27f., 91, 99, 131f.
Matrimony, 28f., 37, 53f., 62f.
Melanchthon, 14, 15, 48f., 55, 85
Military service. *See* War.
Milton, 36, 42
Ministry, 29, 74–91
  appointment to, 29, 80f.
  character indelebilis, 83f.
  degrees of. *See* Bishops.
  examination, 29, 81, 92
  Ordination, 29, 55, 69, 71, 74ff., 81–4
  training for, 29
Modernism, 20
Monastery, 21ff.
Monastic life, 28, 37
Morals. *See* Law.
Music, 96f.
Mystical Union, 52

NATIONAL SOCIALISTS, STERILISATION LAWS, 63f.
Norway, 15, 87, 89, 127. *See also* Church conflict.

ORDINATION. *See* Ministry.
Orlamünde. *See* Karlstadt.
Osiander, Andreas, 48

PAGANS, 37f.
Peasants' revolution, 135f.
Pecca fortiter, 65f.
Personality
  religious development, 21ff.
Plato. *See* Aristotle.
Politics, 142–7
Pope, 25, 32, 53, 91, 105, 108f., 123f., 133, 141
Predestination, 36, 42, 59
Pre-Reformers, 29–31
Priest, 75–7, 80, 82. *See also* Ministry.
Priesthood, universal, 77ff., 132f.
Princes, 21, 29, 126–50
Property of the Church, 28
Protestants, 17f., 97f., 123f., 132

RACE, 34f., 42f., 148f.
Rationalism, 16, 20
Reason, 20f., 108–10, 146
Re-formation, Principle of, 20f., 24–9, 105f., 122f.
  95 theses, 25f.
Ritual, 28, 73f., 91–9, 106. *See also* Adiaphoron.
Roman Catholic Church, 25, 26–9, 31, 66, 75ff., 99f., 131f.
  abuses, 25–9, 91, 105f., 131

SACRAMENTS, 53, 55f., 68ff., 84f.
Schmalkalden Articles, 16
Schwärmer, 13, 31, 102, 123, 130, 149
Science, 34f., 119f.
Sex life. *See* Matrimony.
Sin, 34–8
  original, 38
Soul, human, origin of, 38f.
State, 42f., 126–50. *See also* Politics.
Staupitz, Johann von, 22
Sweden, 15, 87, 89
  Confirmation in Sweden, 51

TETZEL, JOHANN (DOMINICAN MONK), 25f.
Training. *See* Ministry.
Transubstantiation. *See* Holy Communion and Sacraments.
Trent, Council of, 13
Trinity, 44f.
Turks, 64, 102, 104
Turmstubenerlebnis, 23

UNIVERSITIES, 78, 81, 144
University of Wittenberg, 23, 29, 32, 81f., 137

Visitatores, 77, 137f.

WAR, ATTITUDE TO, 65f.
Word, Divine, 68ff., 107–10, 116–20, 128ff.

ZWINGLI, HULDREICH, 29f., 53f., 109f.
Zwinglians, 31

www.ingramcontent.com/pod-product-compliance
Lightning Source LLC
Chambersburg PA
CBHW071437160426
43195CB00013B/1933